I0762402

UMBRIA AND ITS ANCIENT NEIGHBORS

The Green Heart of Italy

Photographs by Judith Goodman & Frank Van Riper
Text by Frank Van Riper

Daylight

Publisher: Michael Itkoff
Creative Director: Ursula Damm
Copy Editor: Gabrielle Fastman

None of the photographs in this book was manipulated digitally to add or remove compositional elements or to alter the truth of the image.

The map on page 6 is intended for illustrative purposes only and may not accurately represent precise geographic boundaries or locations. It should not be interpreted as an authoritative source.

ISBN: 978-1-954119-48-2

Printed by Ofset Yapimevi, Turkey

Daylight Books
E-mail: info@daylightbooks.org
Web: www.daylightbooks.org

Also by Frank Van Riper:
Recovered Memory: New York & Paris 1960–1980 (2018)
Talking Photography: Viewpoints on the Art, Craft and Business (2002)
Down East Maine: A World Apart (1998)
Faces of the Eastern Shore (1992)
Glenn: The Astronaut Who Would Be President (1983)

Also by Frank Van Riper and Judith Goodman:
Serenissima: Venice in Winter (2008)

The mysterious landlocked heart of Italy, the old papal state of Umbria sprawls and nestles across the Apennines mountain chain, a fabulous mixture of vineyards and truffles, high tech and arts festivals, Roman theatres and medieval churches. There could be no better guide to this beguiling region that remains off the main tourist track than veteran journalist and photographer Frank Van Riper, who has been chronicling his and his wife's love affair over the past decade and more with Umbria, the only province in Europe named for the color its rich earth produced.

—Martin Walker, journalist and foreign policy scholar; author of the best-selling *Bruno* series of crime novels set in the Perigord region of France

---

When I see that Frank Van Riper and Judith Goodman have finished their Umbria book, I'm taken with both envy and excitement. Envy because I know that they are serious journalists first and foremost, and that means they have really travelled the backroads, the byways of Umbria to produce this wonderful project. And anyone with a hint of visual understanding will know that beauty—both visual and human—rests behind each turn on the Umbrian country roads. I have spent just enough time in Umbria to know where my fave places are, and can't wait to track down theirs, and compare notes. Frank is right: Umbria is the next big thing, and this poem of love to the people, the rich culture, and the best eating in the world, is coming at just the right time.

—David Burnett, award-winning photojournalist and author; cofounder, Contact Press Images

We dedicate this book to our grandchildren,
Max, Eliot, and Anna, in hope of a better,
kinder world in their future.

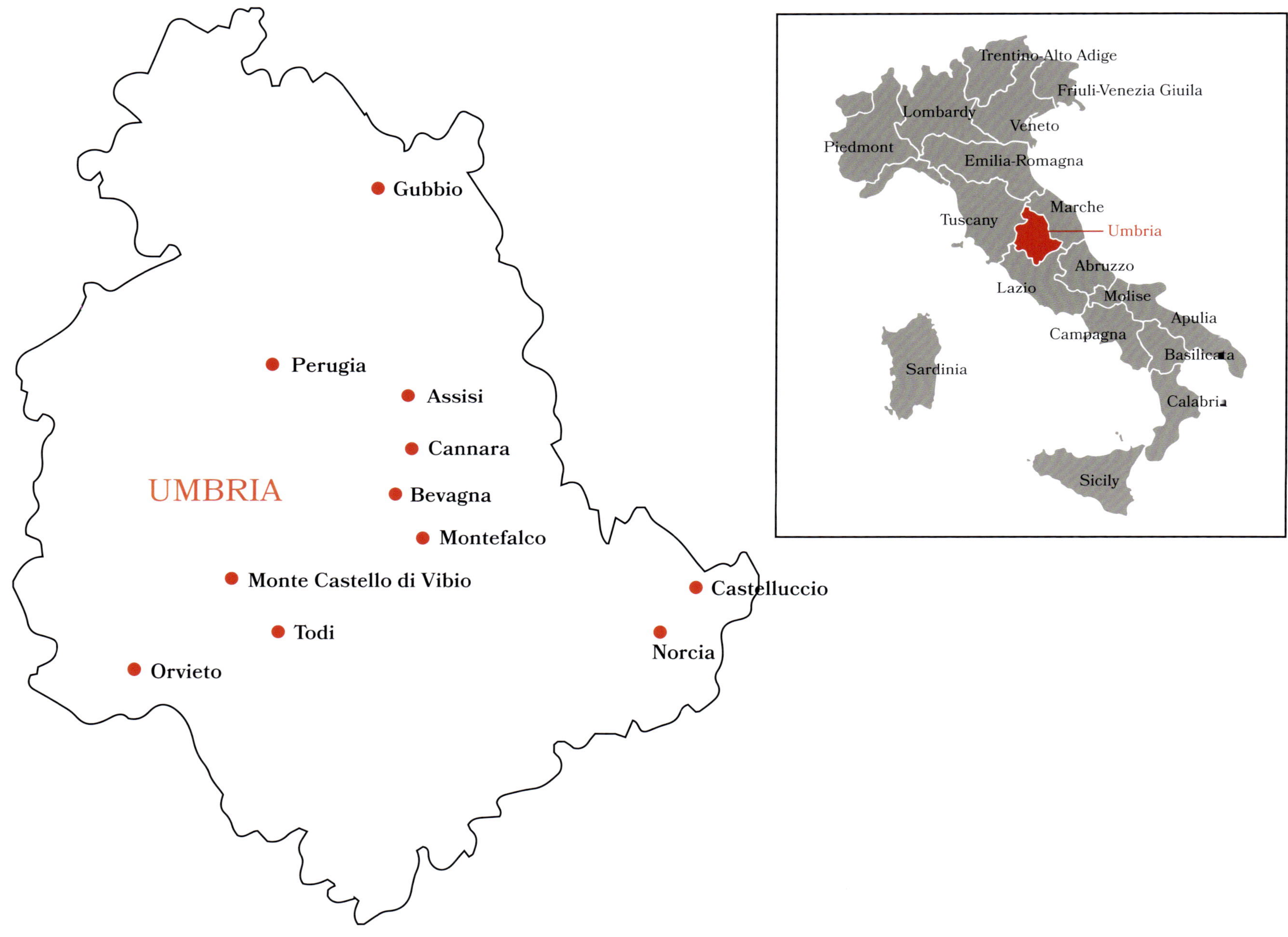
Gubbio
Perugia
Assisi
Cannara
UMBRIA
Bevagna
Montefalco
Monte Castello di Vibio
Castelluccio
Todi
Norcia
Orvieto
Trentino-Alto Adige
Friuli-Venezia Giuila
Lombardy
Veneto
Piedmont
Emilia-Romagna
Marche
Tuscany
Umbria
Abruzzo
Lazio
Molise
Apulia
Campagna
Basilicata
Sardinia
Calabria
Sicily

Introduction

In the seventeenth century, Italy was on the itinerary of every wealthy European or Briton making a Grand Tour of the continent—a trip that could take up to three years. But, for all its appeal back then to Germans, Brits, Austrians, and others with deep pockets eager to study this great country's art and architecture, Italy did not become a truly international tourist attraction until after World War II, when a generation of American GIs came home starstruck.

Despite the devastation of a terrible two-front war that finally ended in 1945, Italy—and, to be fair, France—cast a spell on thousands of Americans who now found themselves able to return to a Europe at peace. A booming postwar economy and low airfares meant that America's large (and war-weary) middle class now could travel to places they never had dreamed of visiting.

For Italy after the war, and for decades to come, that most often meant Rome in Lazio, Venice in the Veneto, and Florence in Tuscany. For France in the war's immediate aftermath, the obvious destination was Paris. (Not for nothing did the 1951 Academy Award for Best Picture go to *An American in Paris*, starring Gene Kelly as an ex-GI who remained in France to pursue his dream to be an artist.)

Umbria, in the very center of Italy and the country's only landlocked region, was largely ignored after the war—which probably didn't matter much to this beautiful and fertile region full of picturesque farms and hill towns that often is called "the green heart of Italy."

But today that is changing. In addition to being Italy's green heart, renowned for its olive oil, truffles, artisanal meats and cheeses, and some of the finest wines in the world, Umbria also is known as "Tuscany without the tourists." It is poised to become Italy's next major travel destination and, remarkably, seems able to do so without surrendering its uniqueness or its charm.

First, you have to get there.

Today one can fly business class direct from the US to Rome and do the same with but one stop before landing at Venice's beautiful Marco Polo airport or Florence's Peretola. But there simply are no international airports in Umbria, save for a smaller facility in Perugia serving international flights only from neighboring countries. And given Umbria's terrain—hill towns, after all, are built on *hills*—it's unlikely that there is a large *intercontinental* airport in the region's future.

With no direct flights from the US, most Americans will fly to Rome, then have to wend their way into the city to the big Roma Termini train station, there to board one of several local milk runs north to Umbria. The first time my wife, Judy, and I did this more than fifteen years ago, heading to a rented villa near Cannara where we would lead a photography workshop, we had to schlep all across the station before we finally happened upon a siding with the local train we wanted. (In stark contrast, nearly a decade later when connecting with family in Venice, Judy and I relaxed in a private VIP lounge at the same train station until our luxury class, super-high-speed, Frecciarossa, or Red Arrow, train from Roma to Venezia was ready to board.)

On that first trip to Umbria, we stepped onto the local train and stowed our luggage and camera bags as best we could. But at least the train left on time.

The trip from Rome to the Umbrian city of Foligno, where we would meet our students, and the van driver who would take us all to the villa, was less than an hour and a half, but—*O Dio Mio*—how the landscape changed.

For nearly an hour out of Rome the somber urban terrain reminded me of Newark. But then the magic happened.

Suddenly, the landscape opened up and grew exponentially greener. Hills and small mountains loomed in the distance with ancient stone ruins—not urban detritus—punctuating the foreground in the lengthening golden shadows of a sunny late fall.

Sheep, goats, and every so often horses, provided living counterpoint to the natural beauty passing before us.

The olive groves were endless.

This was Umbria, and we were dazzled.

I am writing this from our summer home in rural Lubec, Maine—the easternmost point in the United States—where it is hard not to see parallels with Umbria.

The evergreen lushness of the landscape on the Maine coast is spectacular. The quiet of the evenings stands in stark contrast to my native New York City and, now, Washington, DC. The night sky, undimmed by competition from city lights below, glows brilliantly.

But there is something else.

Recall the old saw about the taciturn Mainer telling a direction-seeking tourist, "Ya cahn't get theah from heah." You also might say that, or at least think it, about Umbria. You really have to want to get there.

It may not boast a fashion center like Milan, a culinary mecca like Bologna, or an artistic hub like Florence. And certainly it lacks the political and financial heft of Rome. But what Umbria does have, and nurtures everywhere, is a reverence for *le cose artigianale*, handmade things often associated with the home and the table: world-renowned intricately painted majolica from Deruta and Gubbio, for example.

Umbria's reverence for small things made or harvested well is obvious in everything from its peppery olive oils to its handcrafted chocolates from

Perugia; from ambrosial black truffles to its hard and soft artisanal cheeses and lovingly cured salume served on rustic olive wood boards from Orvieto. These can be adorned by intricately woven linens from Montefalco—and served with a deep red Sagrantino or icy white Grechetto (also from Umbria and truly two of the finest wines in the world).

But above all, and in contrast to so many other travel destinations, Umbria also offers tranquility.

"The word that comes most to mind is *tranquilla*," notes Doug Badger, a former White House and Senate staffer who, with his wife, Debbie, now spends three months a year in the ancient hill town of Todi, in a lovely multi-story house built within the town's exterior wall. "When I'm at the car-rental place [in Rome] and they ask me where I'm going, that's the first word that comes out of the mouths of Italians . . . [and] when people come to visit, they just relax."

In 1996, author Frances Mayes popularized Tuscany for many Italophiles with her evocative memoir *Under the Tuscan Sun*. Now, after a quarter century of tourists flooding the region to excess, the reasonable question might be, "Where's the next Tuscany?"

Husband and wife actors Michael Tucker and Jill Eikenberry (stars of the hit TV show *L.A. Law* and other theatrical projects) already have found their answer. They not only refurbished a rustic farm property near the tiny Umbrian town of Monteluco, in the Spoleto valley, but Michael also wrote about their experience in his own 2007 book, *Living in a Foreign Language*.

"Our goal," wrote Tucker, "was to slow down our hearts and minds until they synched up with the circadian rhythm of the Italian countryside."

In other words: *tranquilla*.

To be sure, Umbria is not composed only of picturesque small towns ringed by ancient walls. Not every town or village is picturesque; some—little more than interruptions along a state road—can be downright pedestrian.

Its largest cities, like Perugia and Assisi, also can be crowded and noisy, especially during Perugia's famed autumn chocolate festival, when seemingly every chocoholic and his or her cousin crams the city's streets as the smell of cocoa permeates the air.

And to be honest, magnificent though its cathedral honoring St. Francis may be, hordes of Assisi pilgrims and the merely curious crowd the huge sanctuary of the cathedral so often that officious guards trying to maintain decorum routinely bellow "No Foto! No Foto!" over a loud sound system all through the day. (So much for decorum, much less silence.) A far gentler experience can be had in Orvieto, where the glorious Cattedrale di Santa Maria Assunta dominates the highest point of the city with its stunning Gothic and Romanesque architecture. And in the church's largely empty and elegant interior no one is shouting "No Foto!"

Still, for every memory of crowds and noise, Umbria and its ancient neighbors offer up dozens more examples of unhurried quiet:

—A slow morning walk in the tiny hilltop town of Monte Castello di Vibio before taking a self-guided tour of the Teatro della Concordia—literally the world's smallest opera house, seating just ninety-nine in what appears to be a miniature La Scala or Fenice.

—Evening cocktails or gelato in the outdoor cafes of the Piazza del Popolo in Todi, where automobiles are largely forbidden and where you can hear yourself think. (To help you linger, some spots even offer small blankets on the outdoor seats, to ward off the evening chill.)

—The frozen-in-amber look of Civita di Bagnoregio, just across Umbria's southwest border in Lazio. This medieval town is reachable only by a long pedestrian footbridge and has precious few permanent residents. It's called "The Dying City," but oh, what a beautiful corpse. And the restaurants are wonderful.

—The winding *calle* of Bevagna that open onto human-scale *campi* that, on almost any day, serve as outdoor living rooms for locals and visitors alike. Its narrow, shop-lined streets are punctuated by kitchen chairs placed for the relaxation of senior citizens, as well as for folks like the postal worker looking for a place to set down his or her bag during a short break between deliveries.

—Rebuilt and revived Norcia, birthplace of St. Benedict, which was walloped by two massive, nearly consecutive earthquakes in 2016. This charming, easily walkable place is renowned for its pork and truffle products, as well as for its Benedictine monastery. Its reconstruction was nothing short of a miracle and, with higher-end hotels now open there, it is likely to attract even more visitors in coming years.

With offerings like these Umbria is hoping to expand its appeal to international travelers. And the Italian government along with the country's tourism industry have been seeking ways not only to get tourists to visit places other than Rome, Venice, and Florence but also to visit Italy throughout the year, not just in the traditionally popular tourist months of summer and early fall.

Such an effort, long thought of but never fully realized, got a terrible jolt when COVID-19 ravaged the world—and all but shut down Italy's, and much of the world's, tourist economy.

For Italy, a forced pandemic-related reboot offered the country a unique chance to revamp its $50 billion-plus tourism industry: to make it more accessible, less environmentally harmful, more user-friendly, less crowded, and more enjoyable for both tourist and host.

"One of our main trajectories is to boost economic activity [through tourism]," Emanuele Manzitti, political affairs counselor to the Embassy of Italy in Washington, told me in 2021. "And on our radar for quite some time has been the idea that we somehow need to develop tourism more comprehensively around the entire peninsula."

"We must promote an Italy somewhat off the beaten track," Manzitti went on, "routes not so commonly traveled, so that when visiting Italy, people can enjoy Italy at a slower pace," staying in an area longer to savor a particular region's art treasures, landscape, as well as its wines, cuisine, and customs.

And with a burgeoning desire, among younger travelers especially, for more low-impact, eco-friendly "turismo open air," as well as what now seems to be legitimate apprehension about traveling on large, crowded (and potentially contagious) cruise ships, the time may be right for Italy to proactively reconfigure its multibillion-dollar tourism industry.

Enter Umbria.

And as new and returning tourists contemplate Umbria and other of Italy's still-hidden treasures, perhaps the most compelling advice simply might be that not all roads have to lead to Rome.

—Frank Van Riper

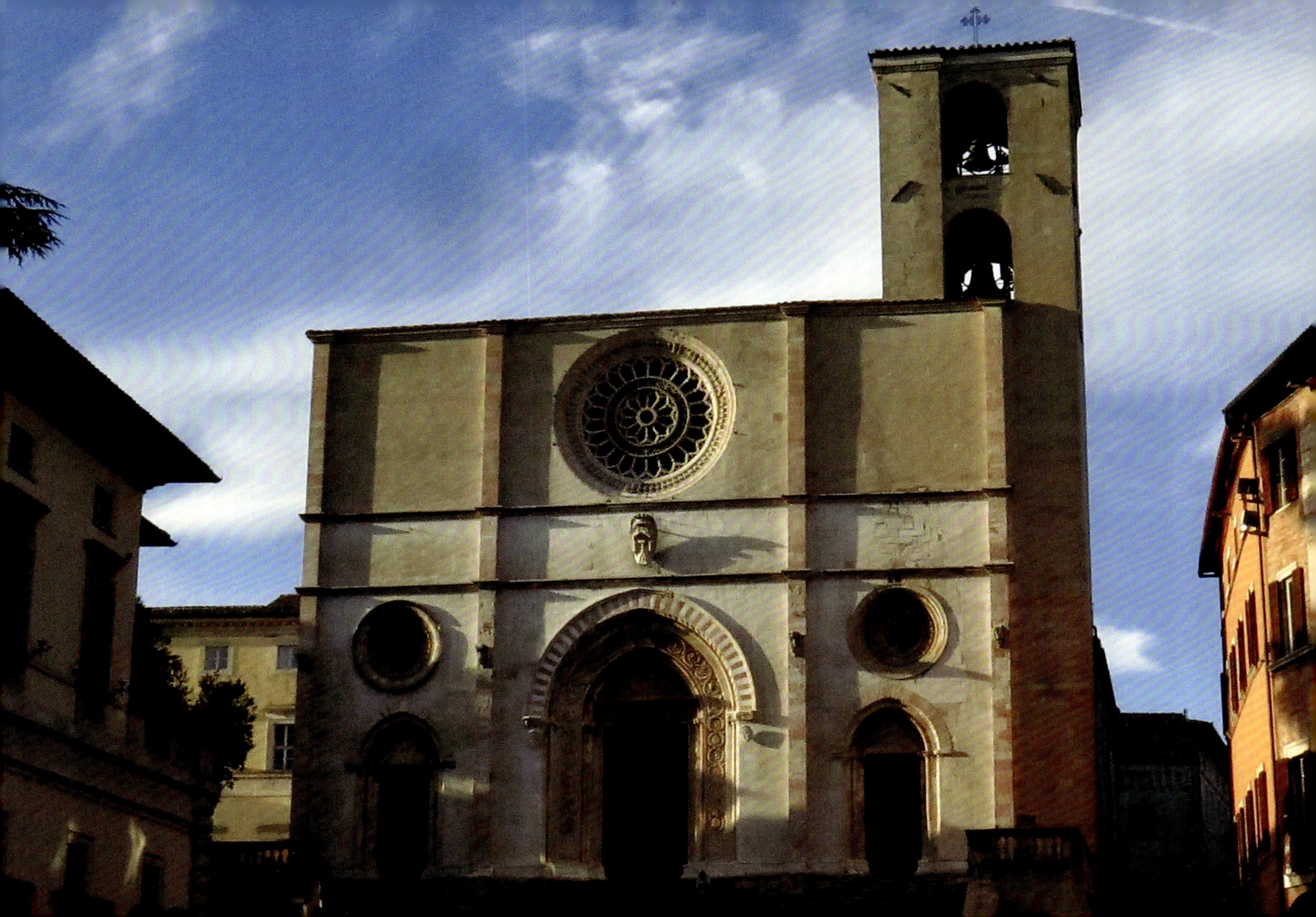

Todi

If Umbria is Italy's Green Heart, sitting in the country's landlocked center, Todi, an indelibly lovely hill town, lies in the center of it all, in the very center of Umbria itself. The newcomer will be charmed by the three sets of ancient walls that ring the town, radiating out with the passage of centuries. The newcomer also will have to learn to navigate Todi's steep hills slowly, like the locals, until a certain tolerance is achieved. It is better, after all, to hit the small, elegant bar of the Hotel Fonte Cesia at the top of the town smiling in anticipation of a well-earned Negroni, not gasping for breath.

The Hidden Jewel at Italy's Center

The 1965 film *The Agony and the Ecstasy*, based on the book by Irving Stone, depicts Michelangelo's sixteenth-century struggle to paint frescoes in the Sistine Chapel when all he really wants to do is carve marble. In the film Charlton Heston portrays the great artist and Rex Harrison plays the "warrior Pope" Julius II, Michelangelo's patron and nemesis.

The struggle between these two strong-willed men—the Pope wants his lasting artistic legacy to be done, and done quickly, while Michelangelo insists the work will be done when he says it's done—takes place, obviously, in the heart of Rome and in the Vatican's glorious Sistine Chapel.

Or does it?

In fact, director Carol Reed's opulent film, which was nominated for five Oscars, was shot nowhere near these two sites. A full-scale replica of the Sistine Chapel was built at the famed Cinecittà film studios on the outskirts of Rome to allow for unimpeded filming, not just of the chapel interior but of Heston on his back painting his masterpiece on the chapel's vaulted ceiling.

And what of ancient Rome itself, as the warrior Pope makes his entrance into the center of the city on horseback after yet another military campaign?

That would be the Piazza del Popolo, some eighty miles north of Rome, in the small, stunning, and remarkably unchanged Umbrian hill town of Todi. Back in 1965, when Todi starred in Reed's movie, tons of soil had to be trucked into the quietly elegant piazza to cover its neat, comparatively modern paving stones. And the austere facades of its ancient buildings had to be papered over with dirt and mock ivy to properly "age" the setting.

But that was all. Todi then, like Todi today, wears its history lightly and well.

With its stage makeup removed and its delicate beauty restored, Todi is one of Italy's, if not the world's, cultural and historic jewels, which far too many tourists never have seen.

It lies in the very center of Italy, near the middle of Umbria, Italy's only landlocked region. The town's roots go back some three thousand years to the early Umbri, then the Etruscans. It has clung to its historic past—Etruscan, Roman, medieval, etc.—while also creating a simpatico, human-scale environment. Not for nothing was it once dubbed the world's most livable city.

As Alexandra Hook, who moved to Todi with her family several years ago from Atlanta, noted, "Todi has its own very special aspects [including a] high concentration of artists and artisans. [There is a] strong sense of community that permeates the town, [and] incredible views . . . the depth of history, the small size and concomitant accessibility to everything, the safety (see 'strong sense of community') . . . and a relatively low cost of living. While, individually, each of these could be found in various locales throughout the world, it is rare to find all of them together."

And certainly, what one also finds in Todi is history, encircled by not one but three sets of ancient walls, each demarking a rich slice of the city's past. And these walls have helped preserve the medieval and Renaissance architecture contained therein better than anywhere else in Italy.

It has one of central Italy's most photogenic piazzas. There is nothing showy about Piazza del Popolo; merely, as one guide says, an understated serenity enclosed by the thirteenth-century Palazzo del Capitano and Palazzo dei Priori. And forming a backdrop to it all is the minimalist facade and rose window of Todi's Romanesque-Gothic cathedral.

The town's most photographed building is just downhill from the town walls: the church of Santa Maria della Consolazione, designed by Cola da Caprarola (in the style of the great Renaissance architect Donato Bramante) and finished in 1607 after a century's work.

Just by itself, Consolazione may be worth a trip. A Renaissance-style pilgrimage church, it features an unusual centralized, symmetrical plan, surmounted by a monumental white dome. This design distinguishes Consolazione from the more common elongated basilica or Latin-cross designs of the Renaissance. And the almost circular configuration of the church gives it both grandeur and intimacy, reminiscent of another great Italian church, La Chiesa di Santa Maria della Salute in Venice.

(An interesting note about Consolazione: for many years twelve niches in the first three apses of the church housed large statues of Christ's apostles.

But, as you will see, time and tectonic plates have taken their toll.)

The best view of Todi—and of its verdant surrounding hills—is from the top of the 150-step bell tower of the church of San Fortunato, sited literally at the top of the town. It's an imposing building (despite its unfinished facade) that houses in an underground crypt the tomb of Jacopone of Todi (1230–1306). Nicknamed "God's Jester," Jacopone was a wandering Franciscan friar and an outspoken opponent of money-loving Pope Boniface VIII. He also wrote lyrical poetry in the local dialect years before Dante did the same thing in neighboring Tuscany. Jacopone is revered in Todi, not just for his gentle (and at times politically incorrect) nature, but also for the fact that he, not Dante, was the first to popularize eloquent poetry written in the vernacular.

But Todi is more than a collection of churches and eloquent clerics.

"The word that comes most to mind is *tranquilla*," notes my friend Doug Badger, who with his wife, Debbie, are Todi residents for several months of the year.

As with many other parts of Italy, Umbria especially, Todi "is one of those places you've never been and felt that you've come home . . . a place where you can walk to the butcher, the handmade pasta place, the greengrocer . . . see people all the time."

Recalling the first time he saw Todi: "I was in Rome one day and we rented a car and drove up. . . . It was in the fog, in November. I'm climbing up the hill toward the Porta Romana and got up above the fog and there was that Todi skyline with San Fortunato and the greystone homes spilling down the hill—you know, everything but the choir of angels."

By the end of the day, Doug and his late wife Dawn had visited a local real-estate agent and seen two properties. "The second place I saw, I bought."

Given such praise, is it any wonder that Todi—with a permanent population within its walls of roughly 2,500, and another 14,000 in the surrounding commune, was dubbed in 1991 "la citta piu vivibile del mondo" (the most livable city in the world)? (In fact the actual accolade, from a University of Kentucky study, described Todi as the world's most "sustainable" city, for its sensible urban scale, but press accounts preferred a sexier adjective, which stuck.)

Still, "livable" does seem an appropriate description. Perhaps because I grew up in New York City, the contrast between the Piazza del Popolo and, say, Times Square, is staggering. First, the piazza is comparatively tiny (maybe a third the size of another famed piazza, Venice's Piazza San Marco) yet also very elegant: a cleanly demarcated (and virtually traffic-free) space surrounded by austerely beautiful ancient buildings and a glorious cathedral.

And unlike Times Square, where you can spend your time under glaring neon while dodging honking cabs and cars—not to mention the Naked Cowboy and

God knows how many panhandling Mickeys and Elmos—Piazza del Popolo is never cacophonous, even during crisp fall evenings when its bars and cafes are packed with patrons enjoying the alfresco seating at the square's edges. Another sign of Todi's small, simpatico size: Whenever I am in the piazza with locals—be they natives or "come heres"—we invariably run into their friends or acquaintances taking the evening air in this clean, inviting setting.

It has been described as a pyramid-shaped town, which is a fancy way of saying that Todi is hilly as hell. You can blame that on the eagle. According to legend, Todi was founded in 2707 BC by ancient locals who initially—and logically—had planned to settle on the level ground along the shores of the Tiber River. One day, so the story goes, while workers were eating their lunch, an eagle swooped down and grabbed the cloth on which they had set their food and deposited it atop a nearby hill. This was seen as a sign from the heavens and, also according to legend, it soon was decided that Todi would be sited along and atop the steep hill.

Steep, perhaps, but with benefits. Notes Debbie Badger: "And then [there's] that stupid hill that I hate, but because I keep going up and down that hill, I don't get fat. I can eat all the pasta I want. Pasta, meat, dessert . . . we don't hold back . . . drink all the wine we want, and I come home [to the States] four pounds thinner."

But if this beautiful part of Il Bel Paese seems charmed, Todi also has had its share of natural disasters. After all, in the summer of 2016, a severe earthquake destroyed the town of Amatrice, less than one hundred miles to the west. Still, fate seemed to smile even then.

As Doug Badger recalls: "The earthquake struck in the middle of the night. Debbie said, 'What was that?'

'I think it was an earthquake,' I replied. Debbie: 'Make it stop.' Me: 'OK.' And we both went back to sleep."

Morning dawned with Todi virtually intact. But not without at least one change.

"As I recall, it was a clock on our kitchen wall that had been making a loud buzzing sound before the quake. Afterward, no problem. Go figure."

Doug added: "After we returned [to the States] the region was hit by another series of earthquakes. The statue of St. Bartholomew in Santa Maria della Consolazione toppled from its pedestal and was shattered. It has yet to be replaced. So there are statues of only eleven apostles in the church today."

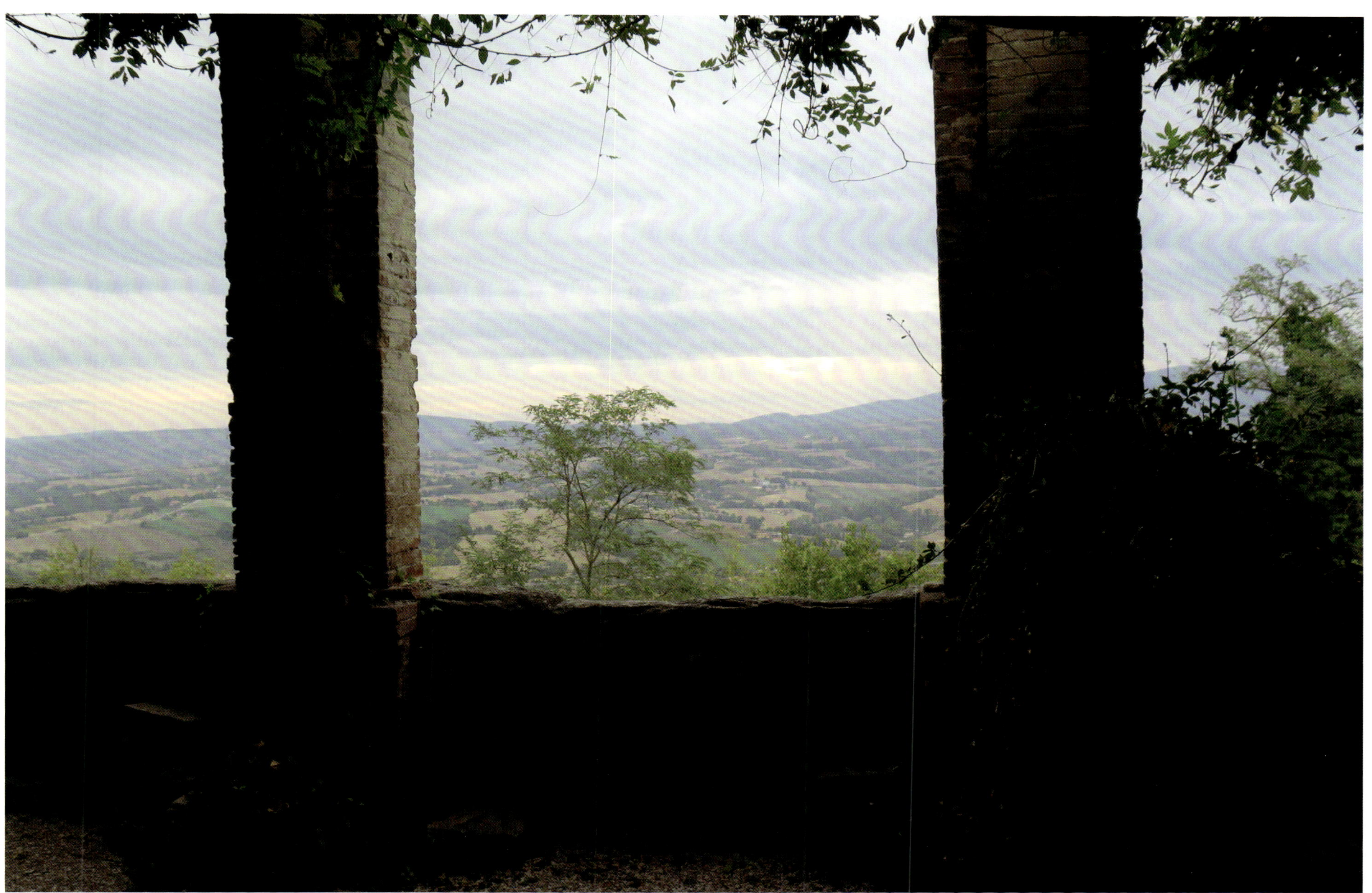

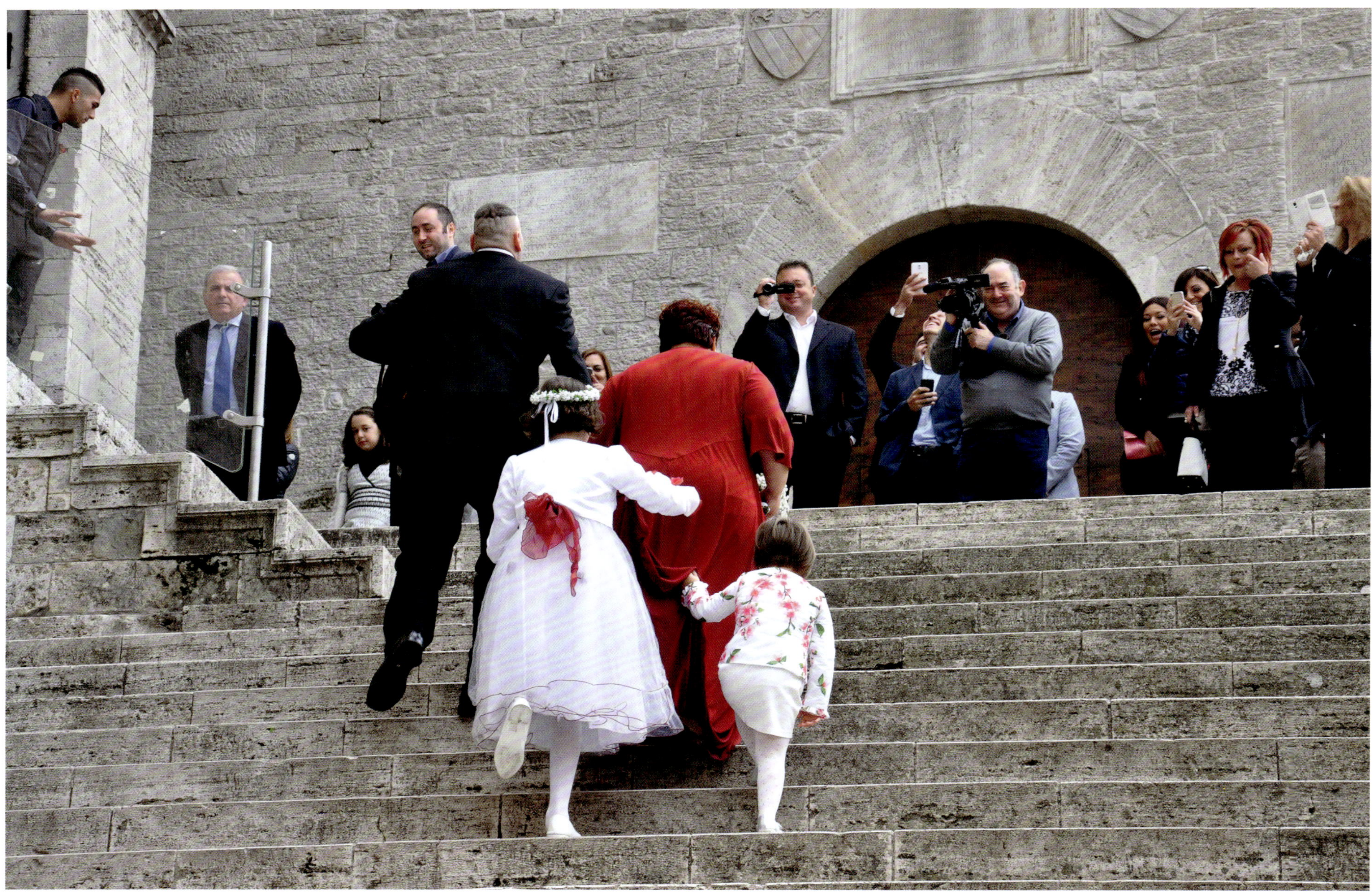

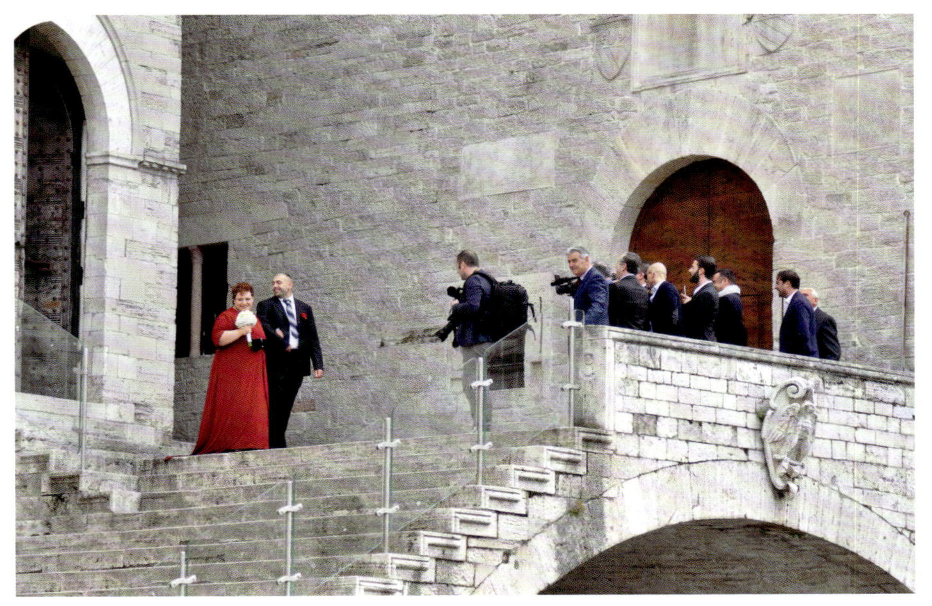

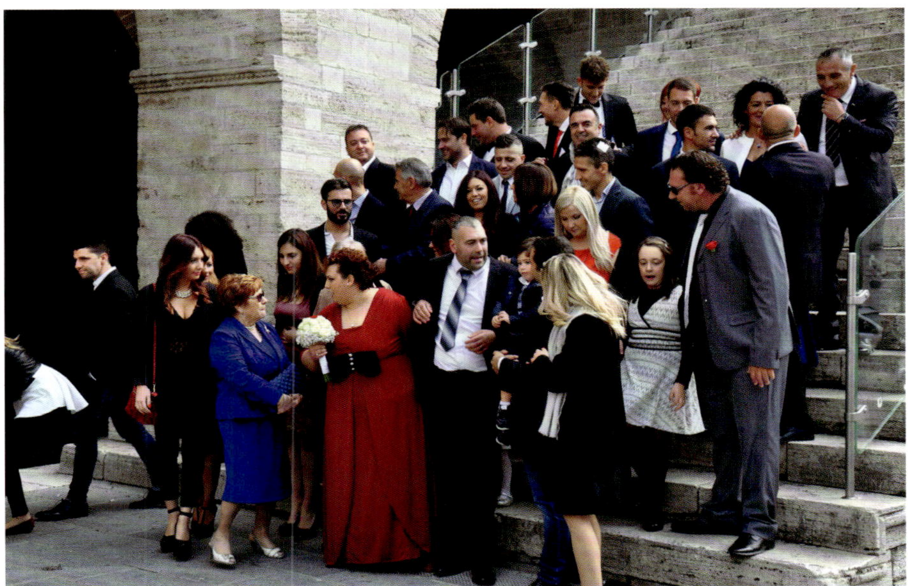

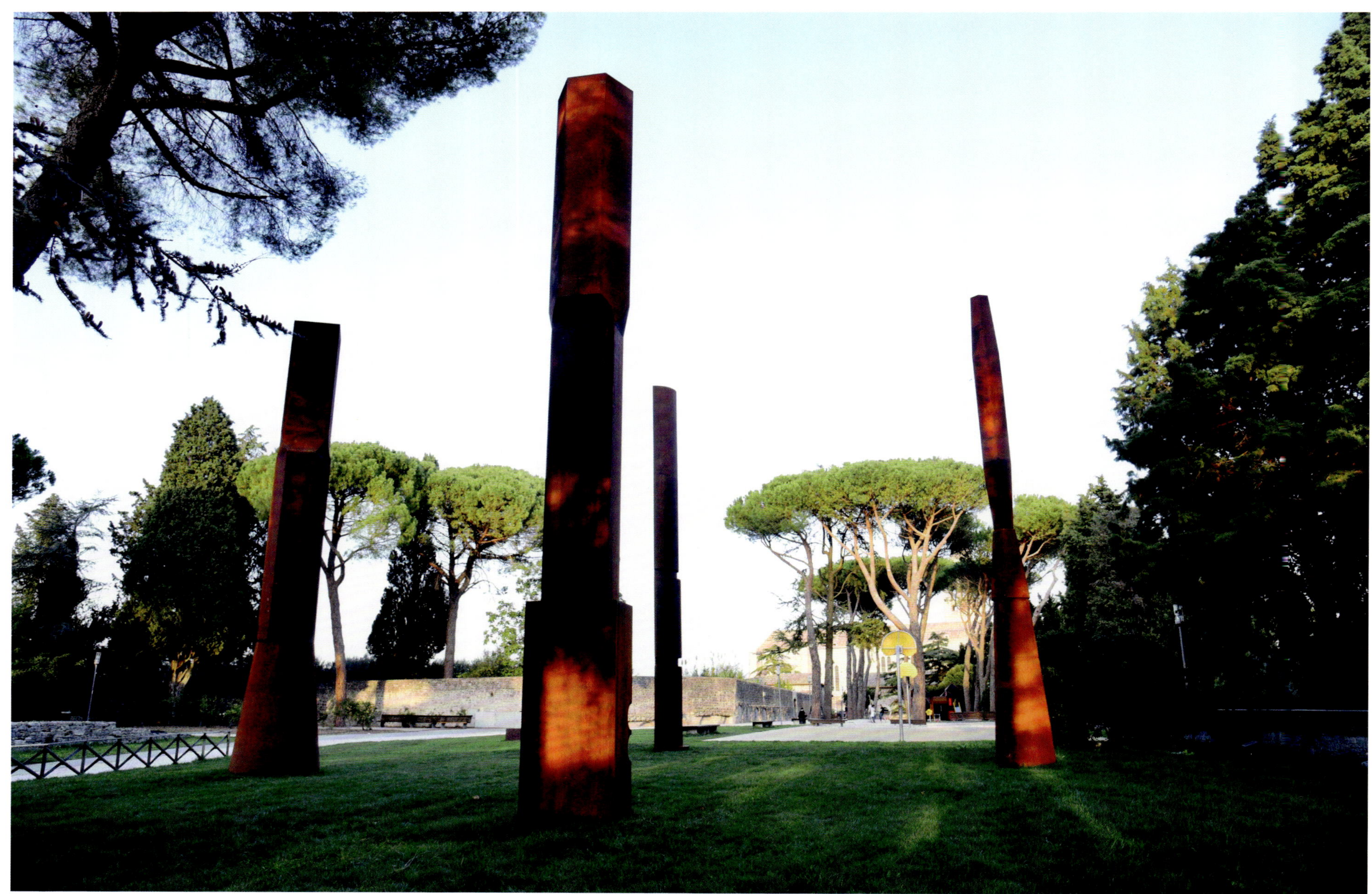

Expat Sculptor of Steel

"Come on," Beverly Pepper said to her new assistant, "we've got to go into Rome. There's a party at Audrey Hepburn's. I haven't seen her for ages!"

This was in 1981 and Pepper, a dynamic, supremely talented sculptor who worked structural steel like it was clay, was talking to Yarrott Benz, a recent MFA graduate in sculpture who had managed to become Pepper's studio assistant at her storied Italian atelier on the grounds of a once-abandoned villa near Todi in Umbria.

Benz, twenty-six at the time, was planning to apply for a Fulbright to continue his sculptural studies in Italy when his dean at Penn suggested that he also might want to contact Pepper. "She might be helpful," the dean allowed. Dutifully, Benz rang her in New York.

"Come on over," Benz remembers her saying. "We hit it off immediately," he said. "She was very welcoming and curious about just a kid from Tennessee." That meeting turned into a six-month sojourn for Benz as Pepper's assistant at Torre Olivola, perched on a rocky Umbrian precipice and looking, Benz recalled, like something out of "an early Renaissance painting."

(Benz, incidentally, did not win his Fulbright; instead, one might argue, he won a Pepper.)

If the name Beverly Pepper (1922–2020) is not as renowned as that of her steel-sculpting American colleague David Smith (1906–1965) or as revered as that of her long-dead predecessor, sculptor Constantin Brancusi, to whom she has been compared, it probably is because she chose to spend the bulk of her creative life in Europe.

And not in Paris or Rome, but on the outskirts of a tiny Umbrian hill town, where she lived with her husband, journalist and author Curtis Bill Pepper, formerly Rome bureau chief of *Newsweek* magazine.

It also didn't help that, in the 1950s and '60s, when she was forging her reputation as one of the finest American artists of her generation, she had the distinct misfortune of being female.

Beverly Pepper first lived in Rome with her journalist husband, where they developed an artistic circle of friends that included, besides Audrey Hepburn, the writer Gore Vidal and legendary Italian film director Federico Fellini. But in later years the couple gravitated to the more simpatico, quieter confines of

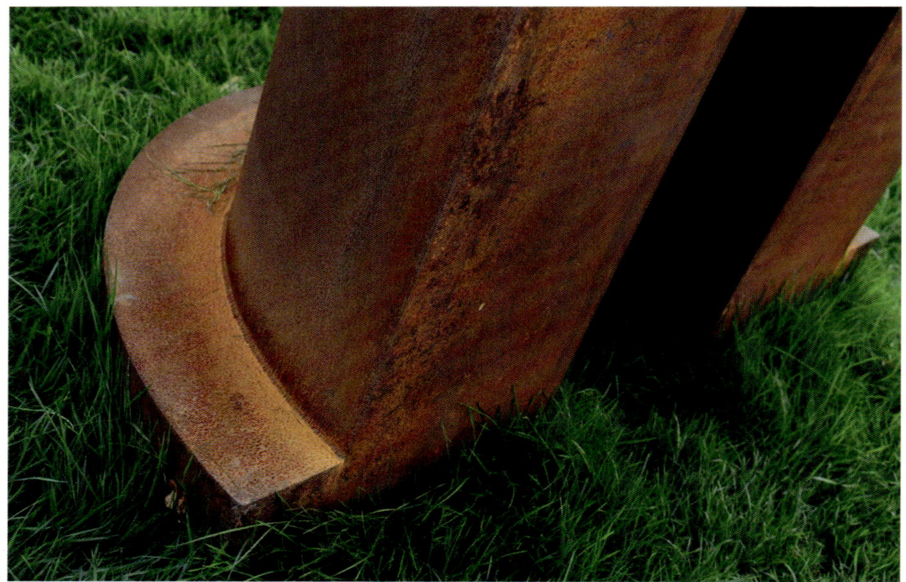

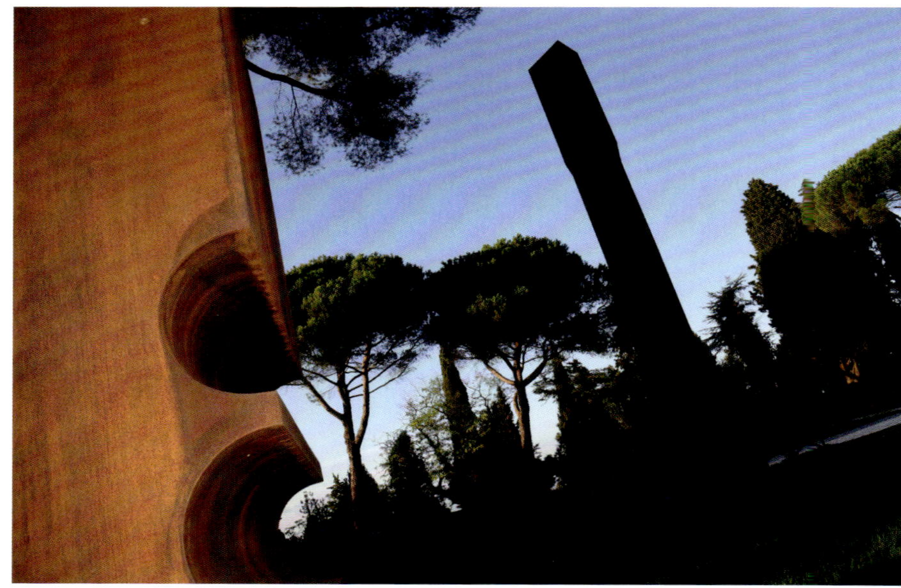

the Umbria hills. Her spacious studio near Todi was her haven, and her love for Todi and its people was reciprocated. Among her many superb pieces, I view *The Todi Columns* as her masterpiece—four elegant ochre columns between twenty-six and thirty-nine feet tall that on two occasions dominated Todi's beautifully austere Piazza del Popolo. Today, this monumental artwork adorns Beverly Pepper Park on the high outskirts of the town, a capstone of some twenty of her works that she donated to the adoptive home that nurtured her.

Born in Brooklyn, Pepper began her career as a precocious graduate of New York's Pratt Institute, where she was forbidden to study industrial design (inappropriate for a woman). Yet she found fame decades later in Italy as a master of monumental abstract sculpture in Cor-Ten structural steel—an unheard-of pursuit (at least back then) for a woman artist. She was a hands-on sculptor, working side by side with her fabricators in studios and factories on both sides of the Atlantic. In every setting her coworkers became like family.

In recalling his six months working for Pepper, Benz, who went on to a career as a photographer, painter, author, and educator, looked back fondly on work-filled days when he would make drawings of Pepper's work, drawn to scale to be used by her and her fabricators. A typical day would start "over coffee in the kitchen," then move to the studio for a full morning of work. "Then at one p.m. her housekeeper Bruna would make lunch—often a simple pasta like shells with ricotta and greens from the garden."

This would be followed by more studio work in the afternoon, capped by a more lavish dinner that Pepper, an accomplished cook, would help prepare.

And so it went.

"The abstract language of form that I have chosen has become a way to explore an interior life of feeling," she once said. "In this way my forms mirror emotional reality."

"Her fingernails were always filthy," Benz recalled, from her work grinding iron and steel surfaces and applying Cor-Ten acid patinas, used in many of her larger works. "The stain is hard to remove, but it didn't embarrass her; rather, her hands were her badge of courage." But when she had to she cleaned up beautifully. (For Audrey Hepburn's party, Benz remarked, she looked quite sexy in her party dress—even to him. "And I was a gay kid in his mid-twenties.")

(This being Italy, one expects to find glorious artwork everywhere, even by non-Italians. And Todi can boast of another expat as well. Viewable today only by special appointment is the Casa Dipinta—the painted house—tucked away at the end of a narrow street and totally unassuming from the outside. It was the Todi home of Irish artist Brian O'Doherty (a.k.a. Patrick Ireland) and his wife, art historian Barbara Novak. Over more than forty years, they turned their cozy multistory apartment into a riot of primary-colored walls and ceilings, merging with perspective-bending sculptural elements, that work beautifully together.)

Pepper could be ferocious in claiming her place in the world of fine art. She hated being referred to as a "woman artist." In fact, she insisted that she always be referred to in Italian as a *scultore*—the male form of "sculptor"—and never as *scultrice*, the feminine form of the noun.

But misogyny and sexism took their toll, especially in 1987 after a devastating, dismissive review of her work in the *New York Times* written by John Russell, a British-born art critic known for occasional—but at the same time deadly—vitriol. Never mind that at the time Pepper was triumphant in shows at not one but three separate New York venues: the Brooklyn Museum and two major Manhattan art galleries. Russell's review was so at odds with other critical commentary about Pepper at the time that one easily could assume that his malice was personal. He died in 2008.

Fittingly, when Pepper died in 2020, having outlived her nemesis by a dozen years, the *New York Times* made up for Russell's critical cruelty. Its obituary for the Brooklyn-born sculptor ran an entire page, lavishing praise on her career and her work and running a color photo of *The Todi Columns* as a panorama across the top of the article.

Nowhere in the obituary was there any mention of Russell's petulant, petty review.

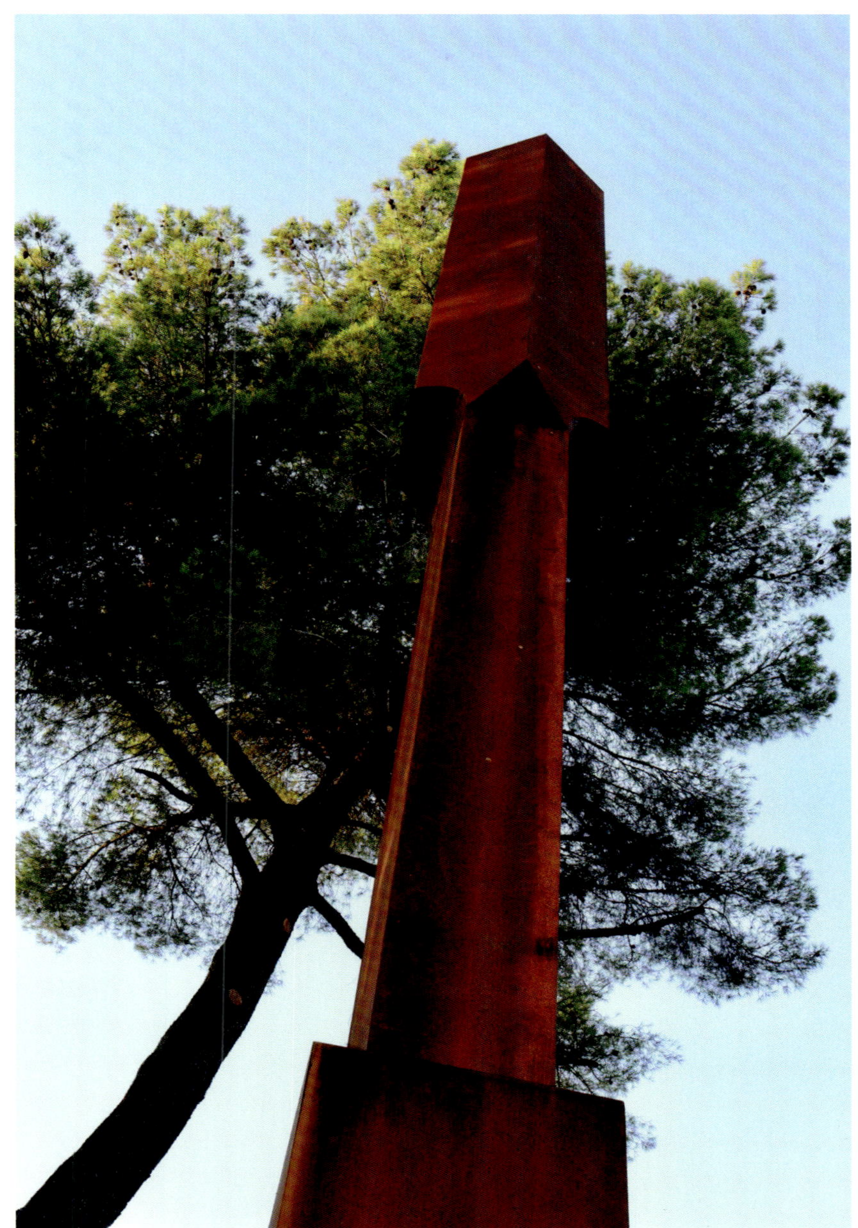

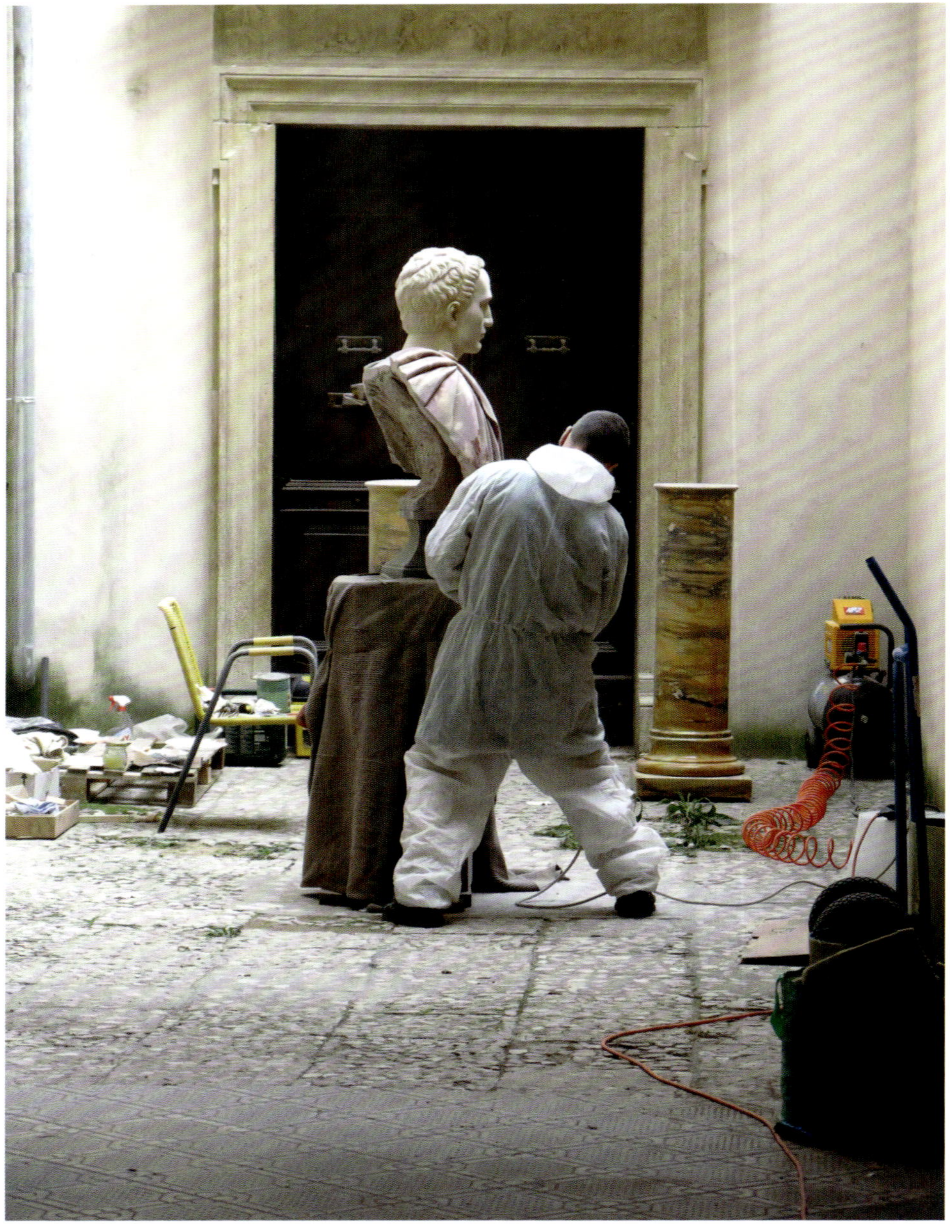

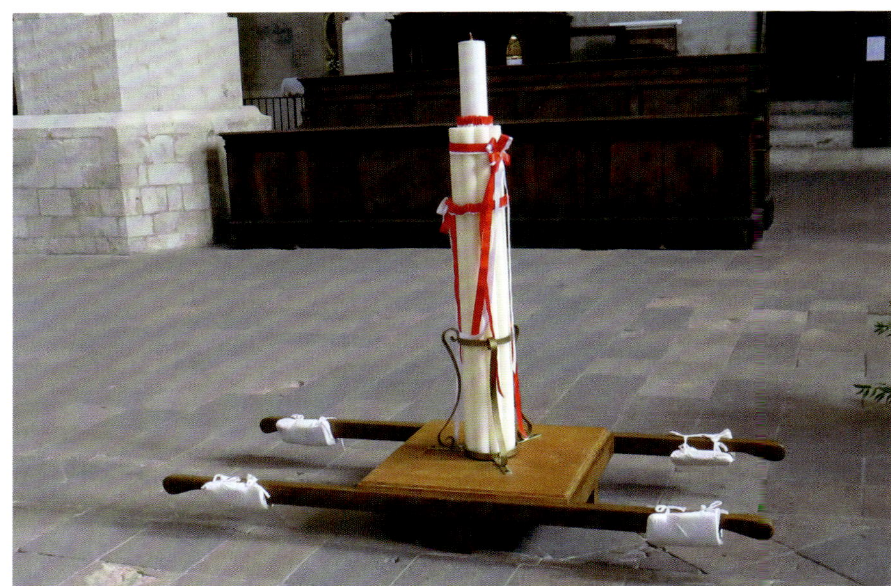

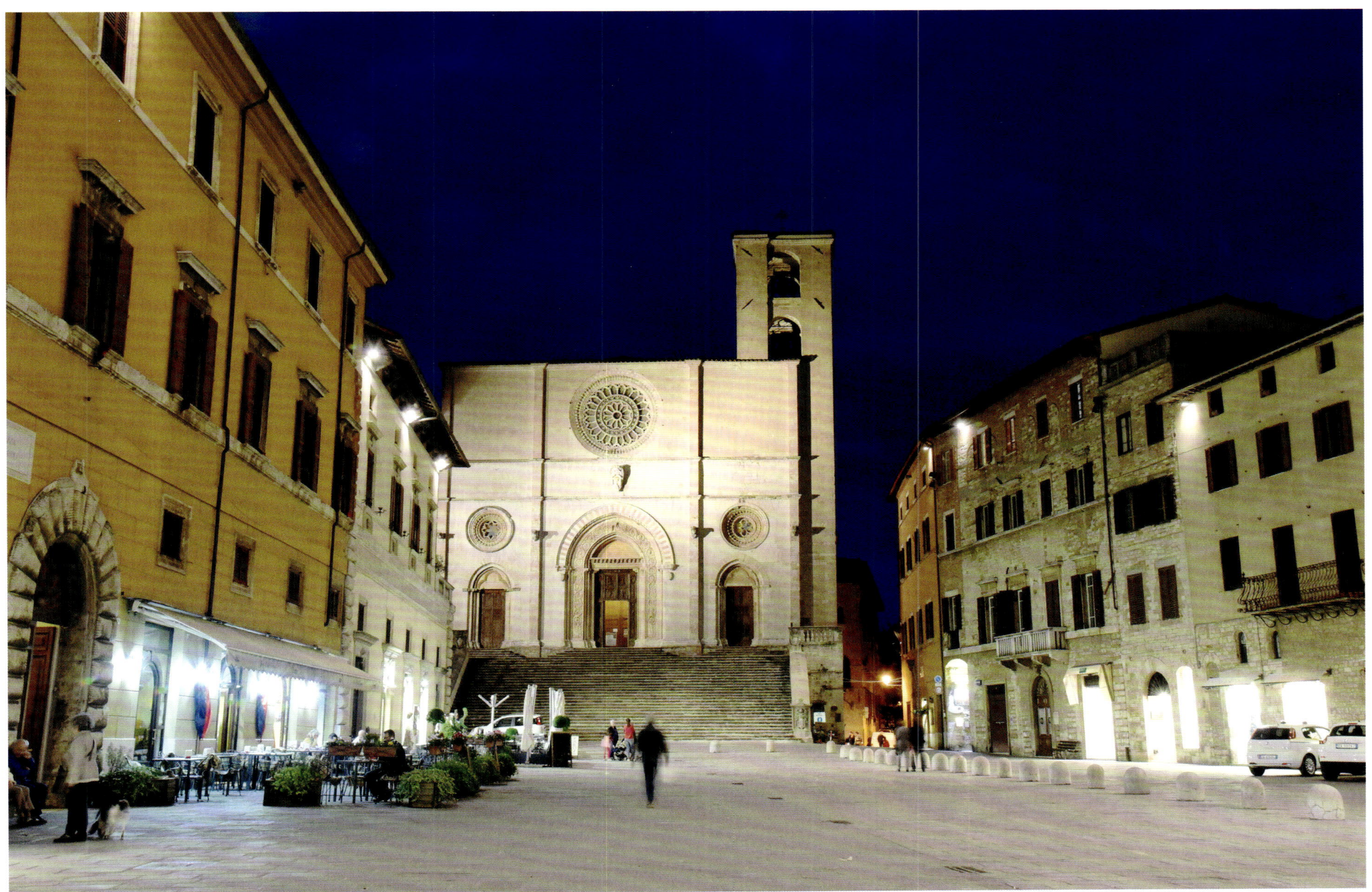

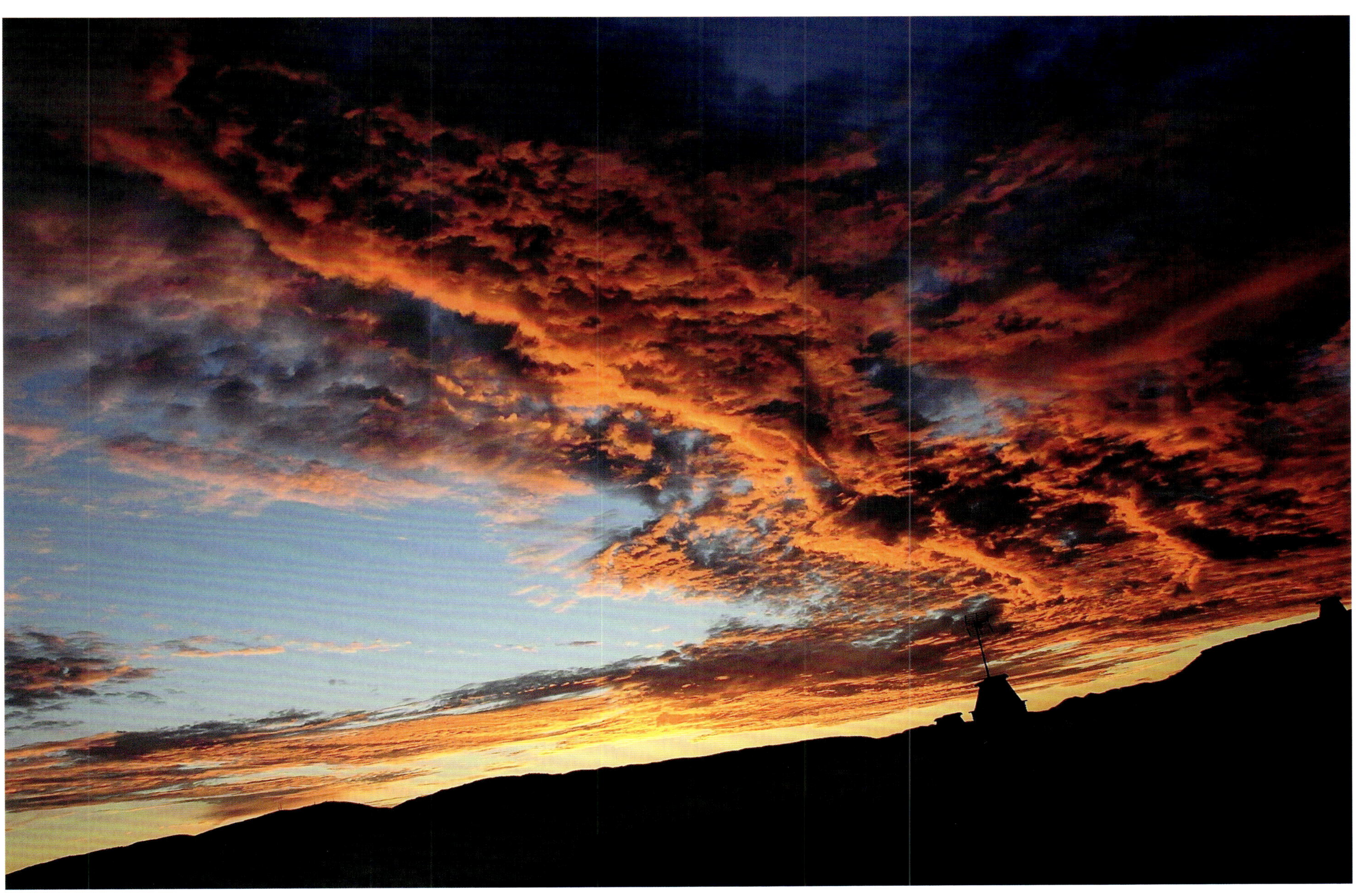

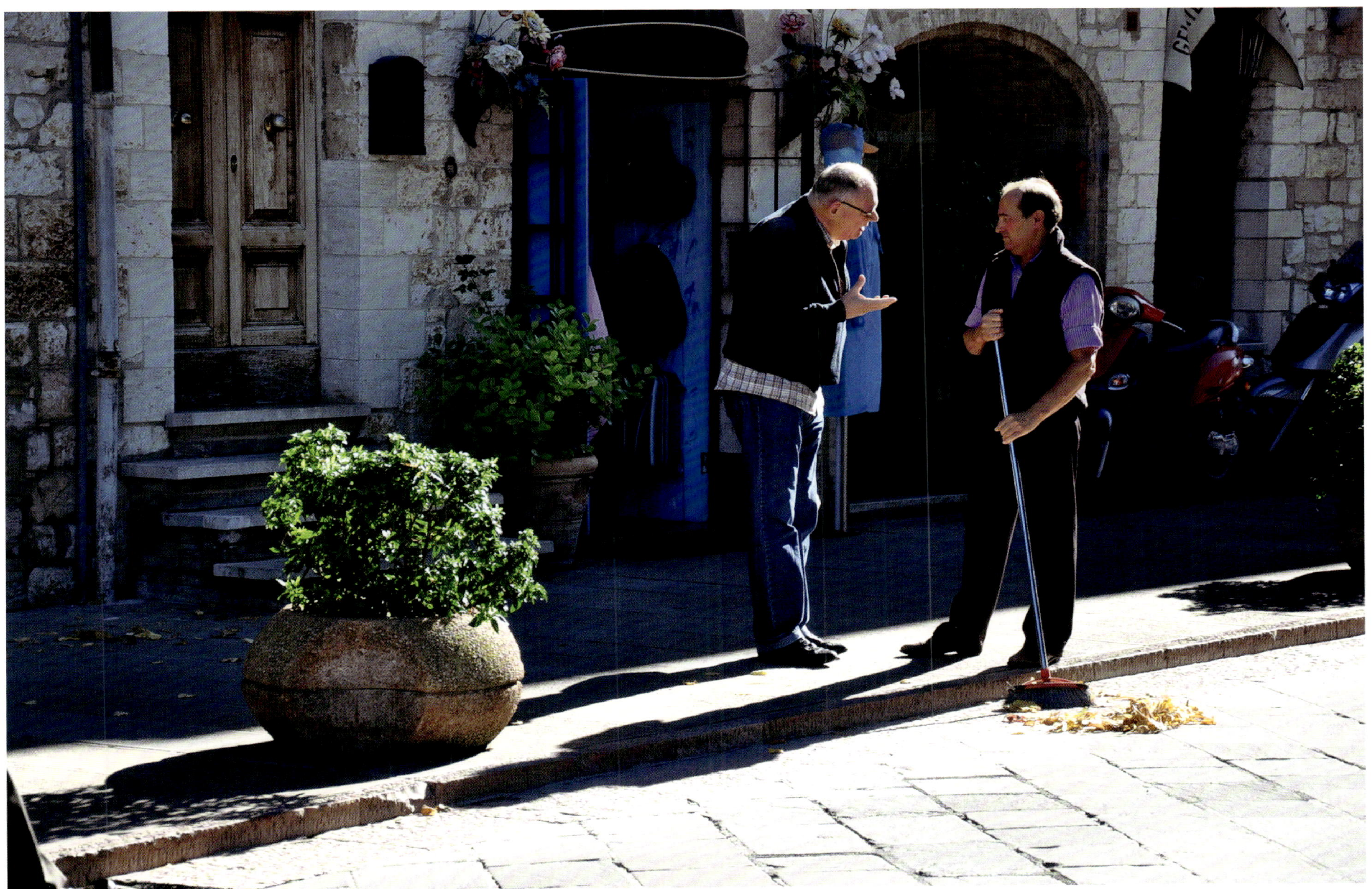

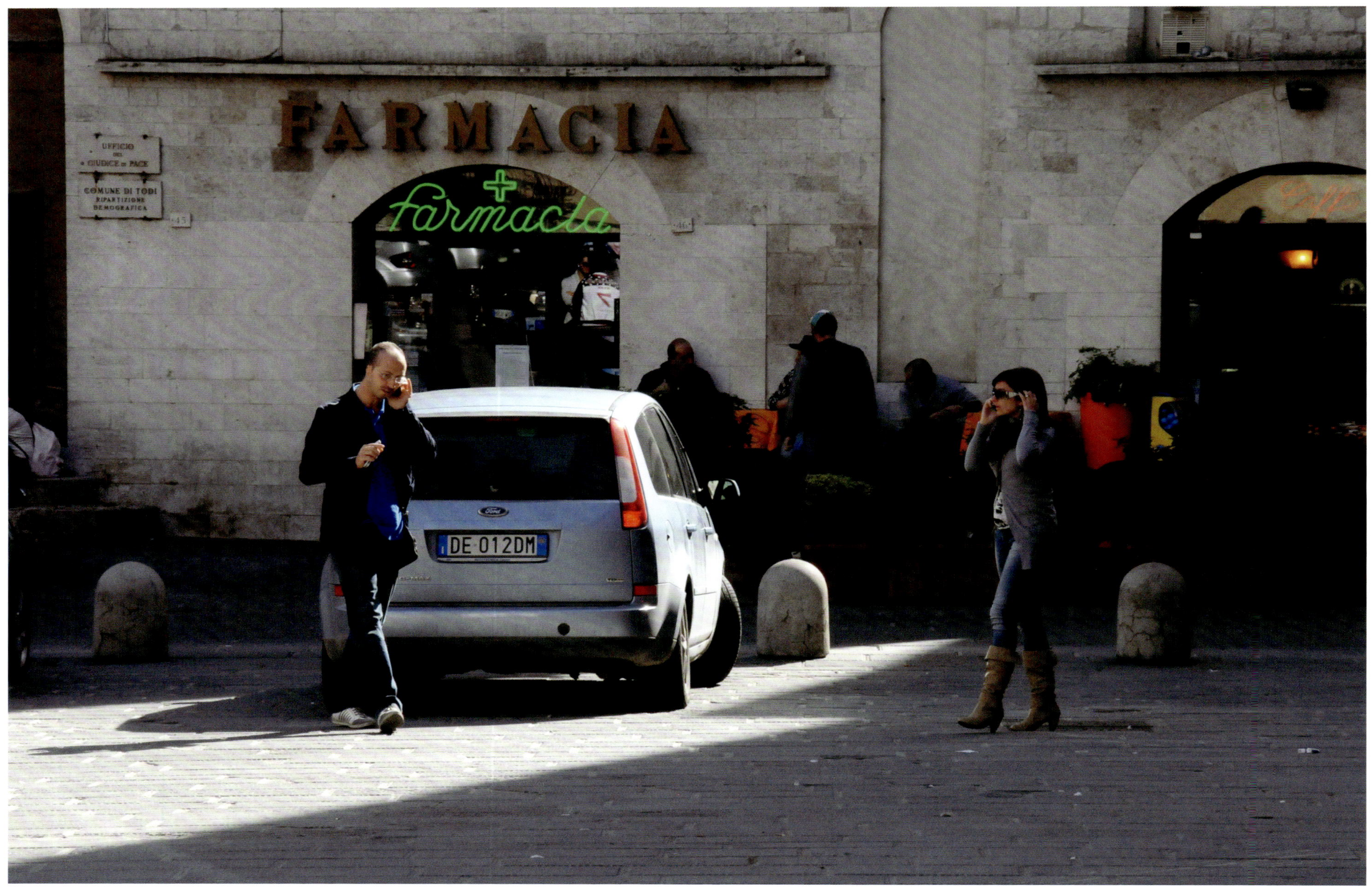
FARMACIA
farmacia
UFFICIO
GIUDICE PACE
COMUNE DI TODI
RIPARTIZIONE
DEMOGRAFICA
DE 012DM

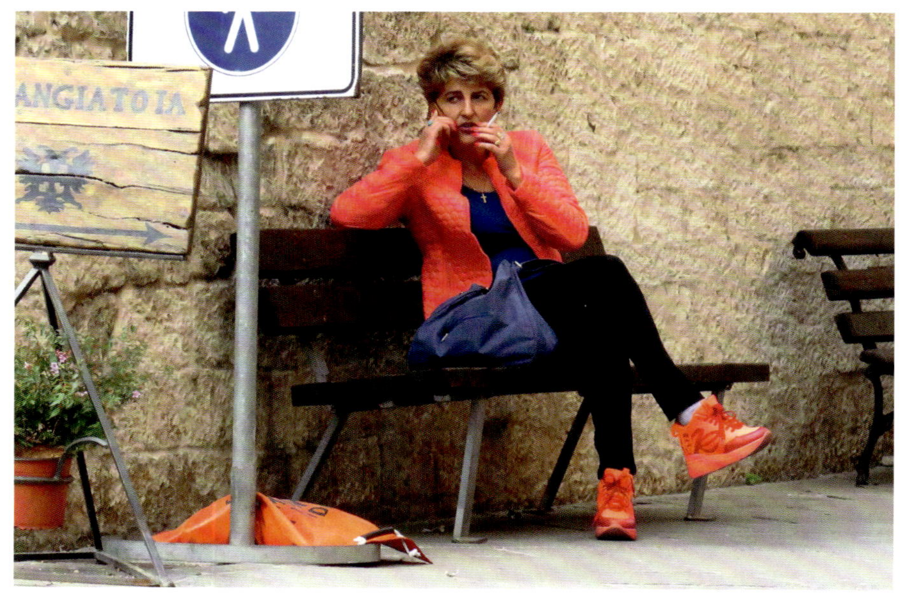
ANGIATOIA

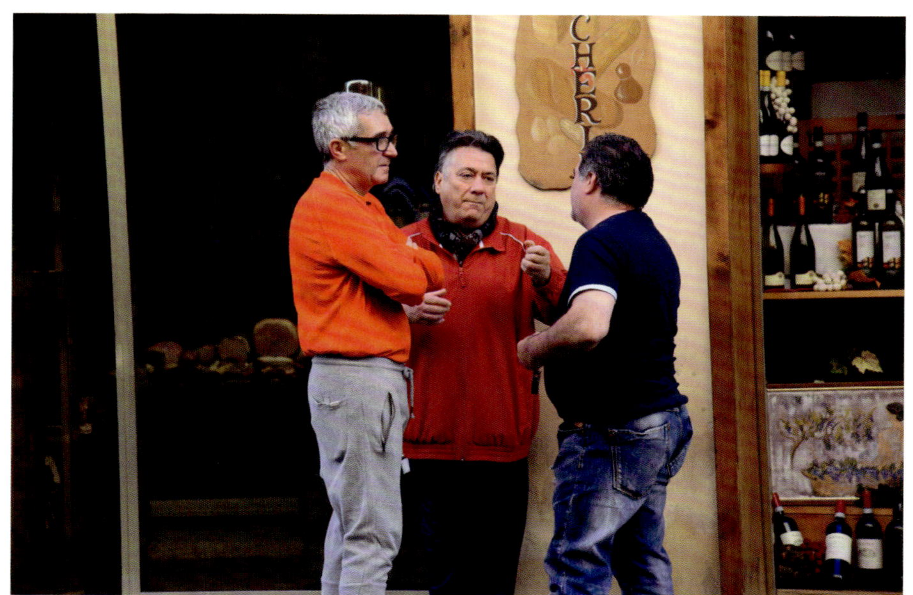

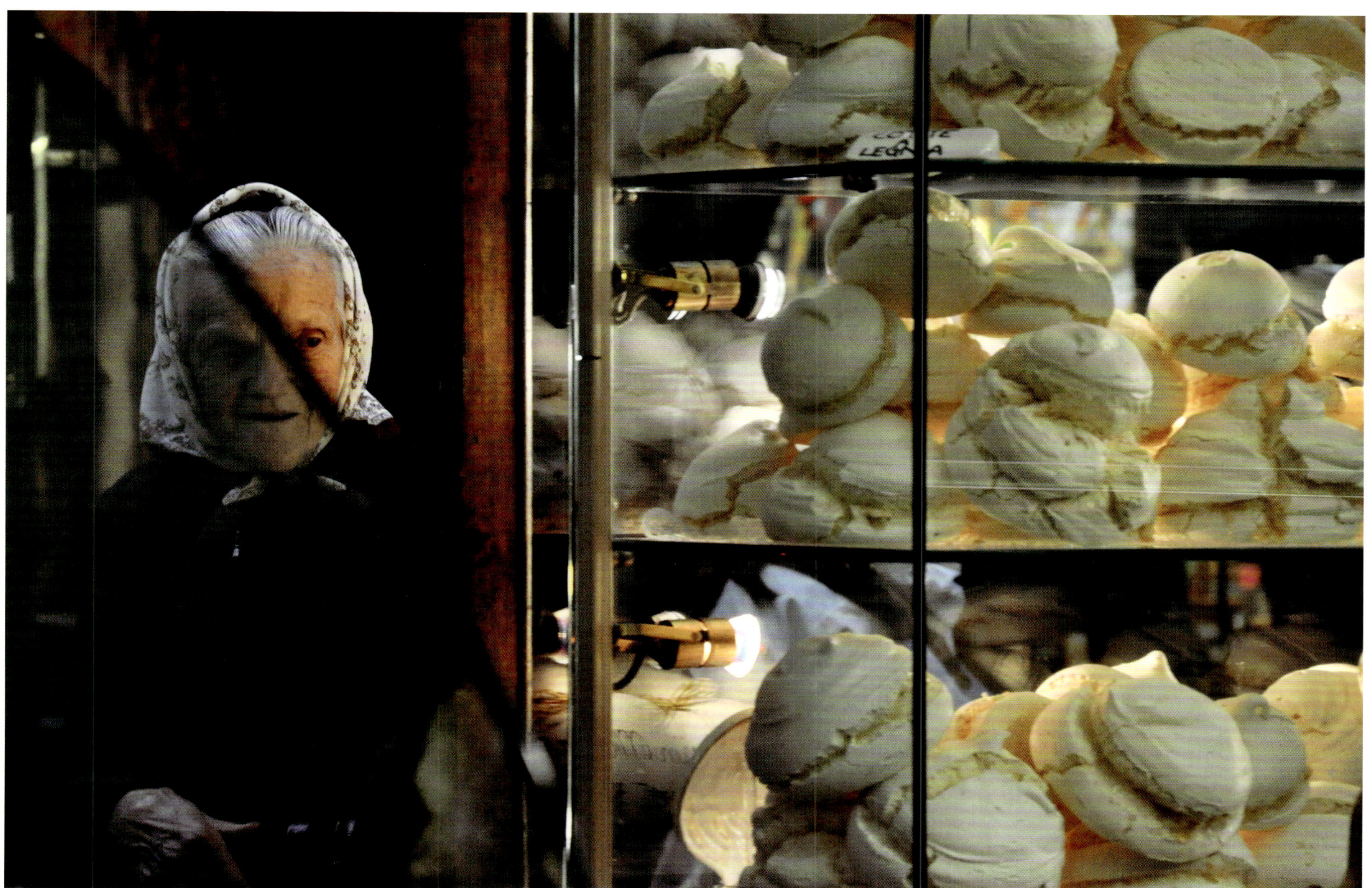

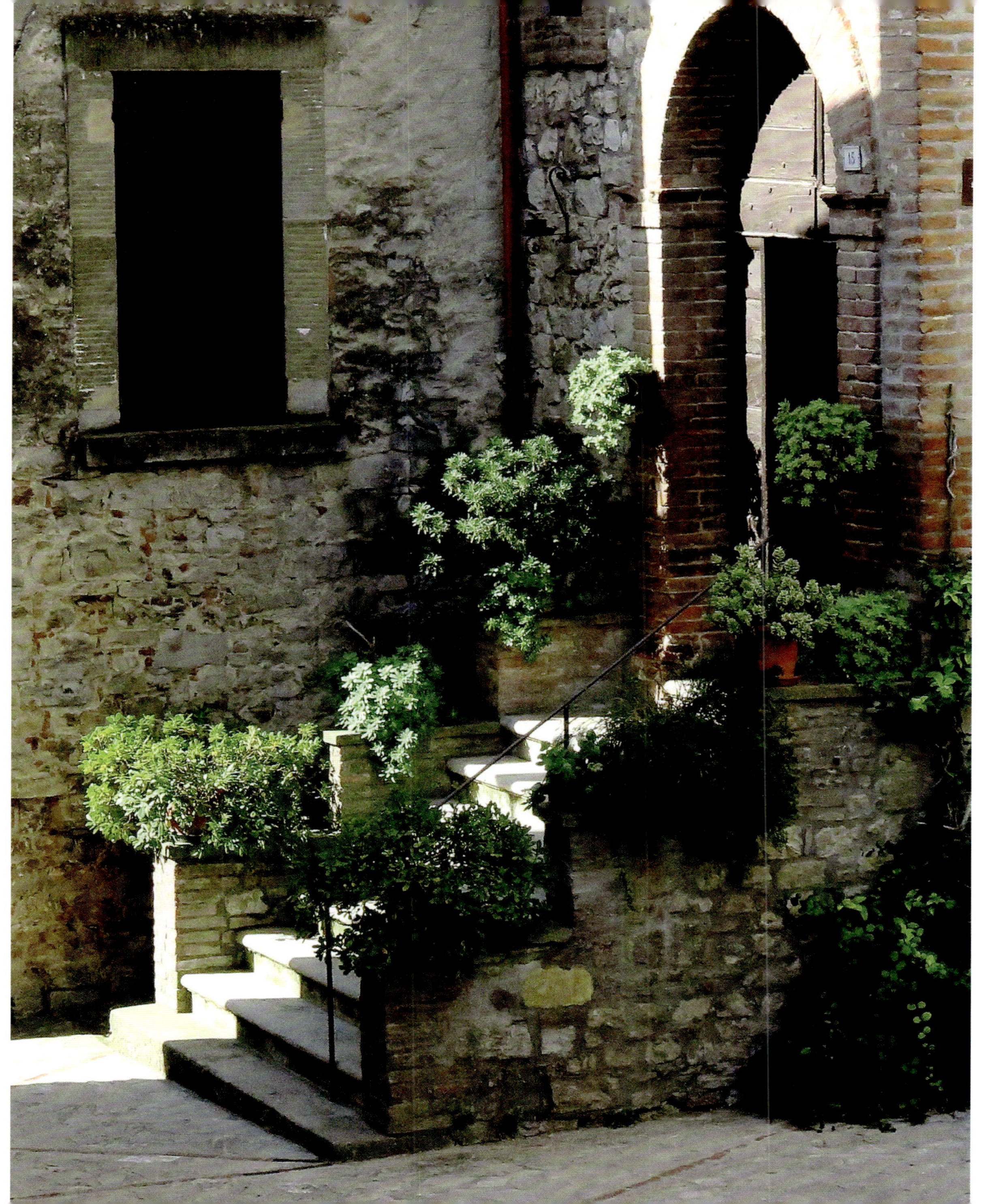

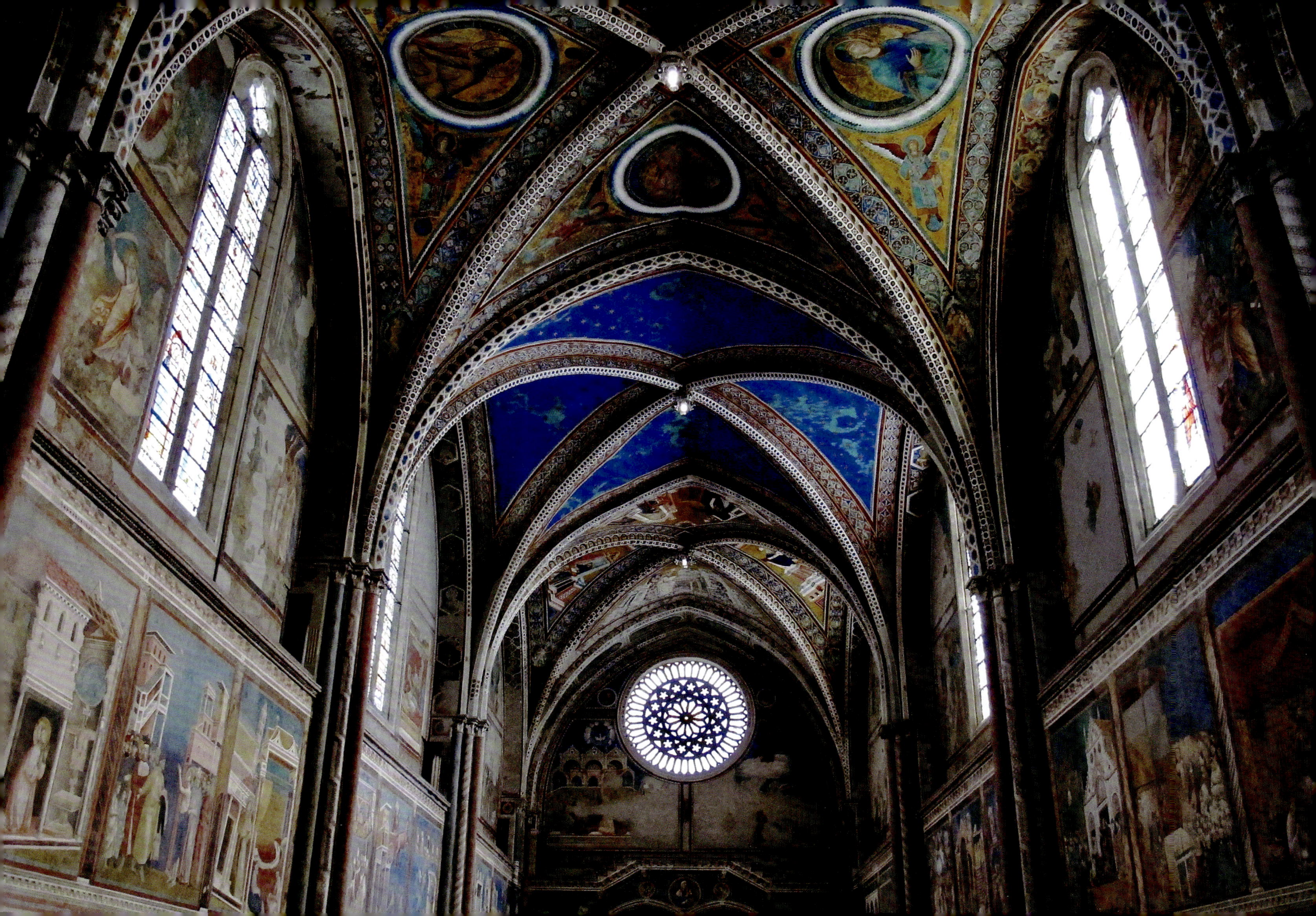

Assisi & Gubbio

Its namesake saint, Francis of Assisi, was a poor friar who spoke to the birds and the animals—and once even was said to have charmed a ravenous wolf. He is honored in this formal and hilly place with a glorious basilica that attracts the devout, the artistic, and the merely curious by the tens of thousands each year. Given Francis's fame and adulation, the town revolves around the saint, and his church holds up its end with a stunning vaulted ceiling decorated in brilliant blues and gold, not to mention Giotto's series of huge paintings depicting Francis's colorful life during which he renounced his father's wealth to become an ascetic and a wandering mendicant. The saint's body is buried in a subterranean vault in the basilica, making it one of the Catholic Church's most venerated sites. But to understand Francis himself, one first must go to Gubbio.

Finding Gubbio: Where Even the Wolf Is Friendly

You've heard of the Ides of March.

Probably, too, the White Cliffs of Dover. But, honestly, the Wolf of Gubbio?

You'd be forgiven for not knowing about the Wolf—he lived centuries ago, during the time of St. Francis of Assisi. The gentle saint looms large in the beast's legend because the two wound up becoming friends—or so the story goes.

You also could be forgiven for dismissing the legend of Francis turning the ravenous wolf into Gubbio's faithful protector as just so much religious hagiography.

But, in fact, based on comparatively recent evidence, the story just may be true.

Fascinating, like so many other things in this small, lovely, and very ancient Umbrian hill town.

Gubbio may not be on every tourist's radar, but I am glad it was on ours more than a decade ago when we first started touring Umbria leading photo workshops. We'd never heard of it, but friends put it on our itinerary as a place where we could see Umbria's famed majolica pottery being made and, more important, decorated.

When we got there we also found (besides gorgeous *ceramiche*) some of the oldest ruins in the country, including a Roman amphitheater dating back to the first century AD. This huge open-air space may call to mind a smaller version of the Colosseum in Rome, but what struck Judy and me—as well as our photography students—as we roamed all over it with our cameras was that we had the place pretty much to ourselves. (Try experiencing that during high season at the Roman Colosseum as you dodge dozens of umbrella-toting tour guides and their long lines of camera-toting clients.)

All of which points up Gubbio's uniqueness. Like much of Umbria, Gubbio is never boastful or self-consciously gaudy (except perhaps at Christmas, when it displays the world's largest Christmas tree, or when, every May, it stages a bizarre race of shoulder-carried statues of three huge saints, calling to mind run-the-bases footraces with outsize team mascots in American baseball parks). With its narrow streets and medieval buildings of dark grey stone, Gubbio is one of the largest and best-preserved medieval towns in all of Italy.

One certainly gets the feeling of ancient art and artisans when touring the famed ceramiche Biagioli (www.ceramichebiagioli.com).

Of all the studios in Italy producing majolica—ornately decorated ceramicware that dates back to fifteenth-century Majorca in Spain—Biagioli may be the most impressive, and most ornate. Its potters produce an astounding array of objects, from coffee mugs to huge floor-standing vases and vessels. And a small coterie of painters, almost always women, decorates the objects totally by hand using techniques that go back centuries. On one of our visits a potter produced a foot-high vase, staring intently at his wheel as the clay pot took form under his hands. Before we could admire the finished object, he took a wire and split it down the middle as we all gasped.

Smiling (he'd done this before, I am sure), the potter displayed the cleft pot to show how its rounded sides were of equal thickness top to bottom: the mark of a master craftsman.

Arguably, one of Gubbio's most charming and unusual attractions is its *funivia*. If you are fleet of foot and not faint of heart it is the perfect mode of transport to a stunning view from one of Gubbio's highest points.

Sure, other Italian hill towns have more conventional ways of scaling heights without having to endlessly schlep on foot. Perugia, for example, has an incredible network of underground escalators and walkways built into its hillsides that let you experience its ancient subterranean buildings. They call to mind moving airport walkways, only Perugia's go up and down, not from Concourse A to Concourse B. And in Todi and Orvieto, you can ride in little funicular cars that will bring you from the lower parts of the town to the town center above, and vice versa.

But in Gubbio, think of riding in human-scale birdcages that barely can fit two people. You'll be standing up during the ride—it's eight minutes each way—but to do that you have to jump into the cage *while it still is moving*, then hop out of the cage the same way at the end. Fun, no?

In fact, it is. There are hardy young men to help you, as well as to slow down the cages as you get on and off. And when you do reach the top, there

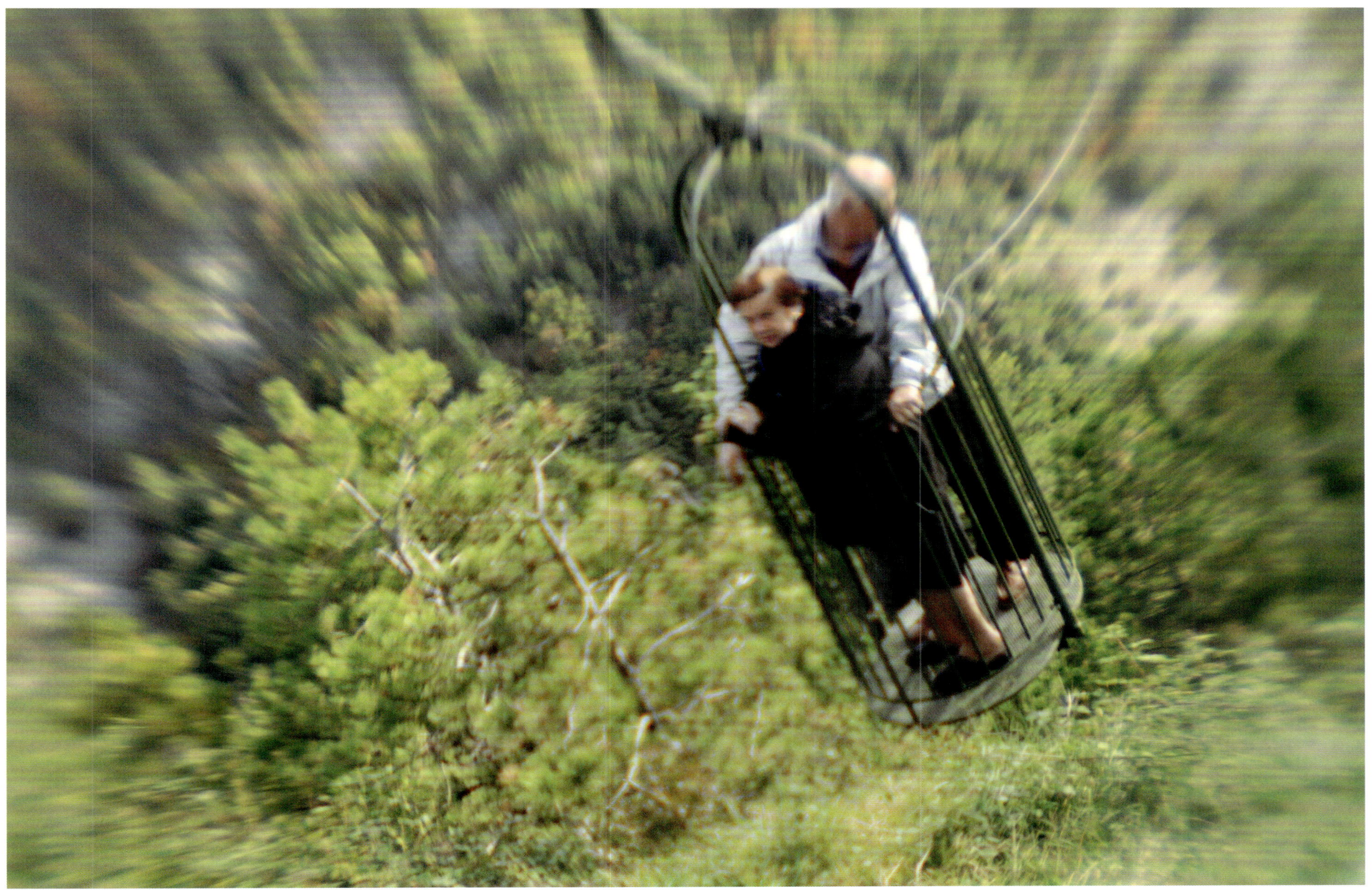

is a large terrace from which to enjoy the view. But the real find for us was a first-rate restaurant and bar that combined wonderful food with gorgeous views that made you think you were in a miniature version of Biarritz.

Hillsides also figure into Gubbio's claim of having what Guinness World Records proclaims is the world's largest Christmas tree.

Since 1981 Gubbio has celebrated the holidays with the enormous tree, which in fairness might better be described as the world's largest illuminated outline of a Christmas tree on a mountainside. But no matter. Guinness awarded Gubbio the title in 1991, and it's unlikely that any other place will top it. The tree, after all, *is* huge—and impressive, especially when viewed from the bottom of the town, extending 2,130 feet all the way up Mount Ingino to the base of the basilica devoted to the town's patron saint, Sant'Ubaldo. The massive lighting display uses some 3,000 colorful lights and more than five miles of electrical cable. At night the Christmas tree is visible from thirty miles away. So famous has the tree become that on two separate occasions the Pope has lit the holiday display remotely from the Vatican, using a tablet computer: Benedict in 2011; Francis in 2014.

Perhaps not as famous as the Christmas tree, but venerated nonetheless, is Gubbio's gentle wolf.

The story dates back to the thirteenth century and the time of St. Francis. Legend says that a huge wolf, injured and unable to hunt, terrorized the walled town of Gubbio, first by eating livestock, then by killing a shepherd and later the hunters who had been sent to dispatch it. The town contacted Francis in Assisi and pleaded for help. The friar agreed to intercede and, again according to legend, persuaded the wolf to change his ways simply by speaking gently to him:

"Brother wolf," Francis is said to have declared, "thou hast done much evil in this land, destroying and killing the creatures of God without his permission; yea, not animals only hast thou destroyed, but thou hast even dared to devour men, made after the image of God. . . . All men cry out against thee, the dogs pursue thee, and all the inhabitants of this city are thy enemies; but I will make peace between them and thee, O brother wolf, if so be thou no more offend them, and they shall forgive thee all thy past offences, and neither men nor dogs shall pursue thee anymore."

According to accounts of the time, the wolf bowed its head, laid its paw in the friar's hand, and submitted to Francis, completely at his mercy. For the next two years, until the wolf's death, it protected the town and was able to survive on the food provided by its grateful inhabitants.

A feel-good story to be sure. But true?

It was said that Gubbio gave the wolf an honorable burial and later built the Church of Saint Francis of the Peace at the site. As centuries passed the story of the transformed Wolf of Gubbio lived as a legend—but little more—until 1872. Then, during renovations to St. Francis's church, the skeleton of a large wolf, apparently several centuries old, was found under a slab near the church wall and reburied inside.

What possible reason could the church have had to bury the carcass of a wolf near consecrated ground?

Fascinating.

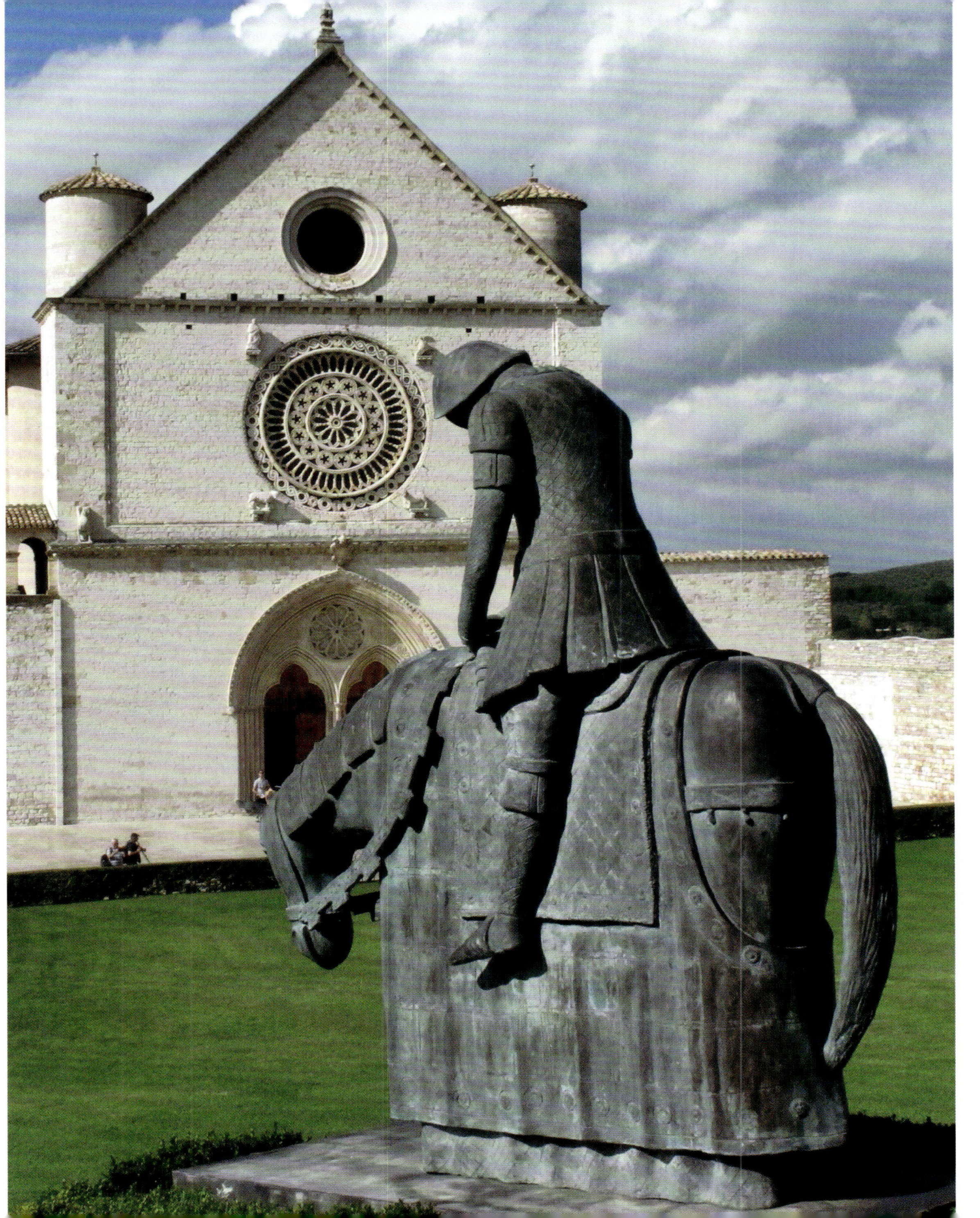

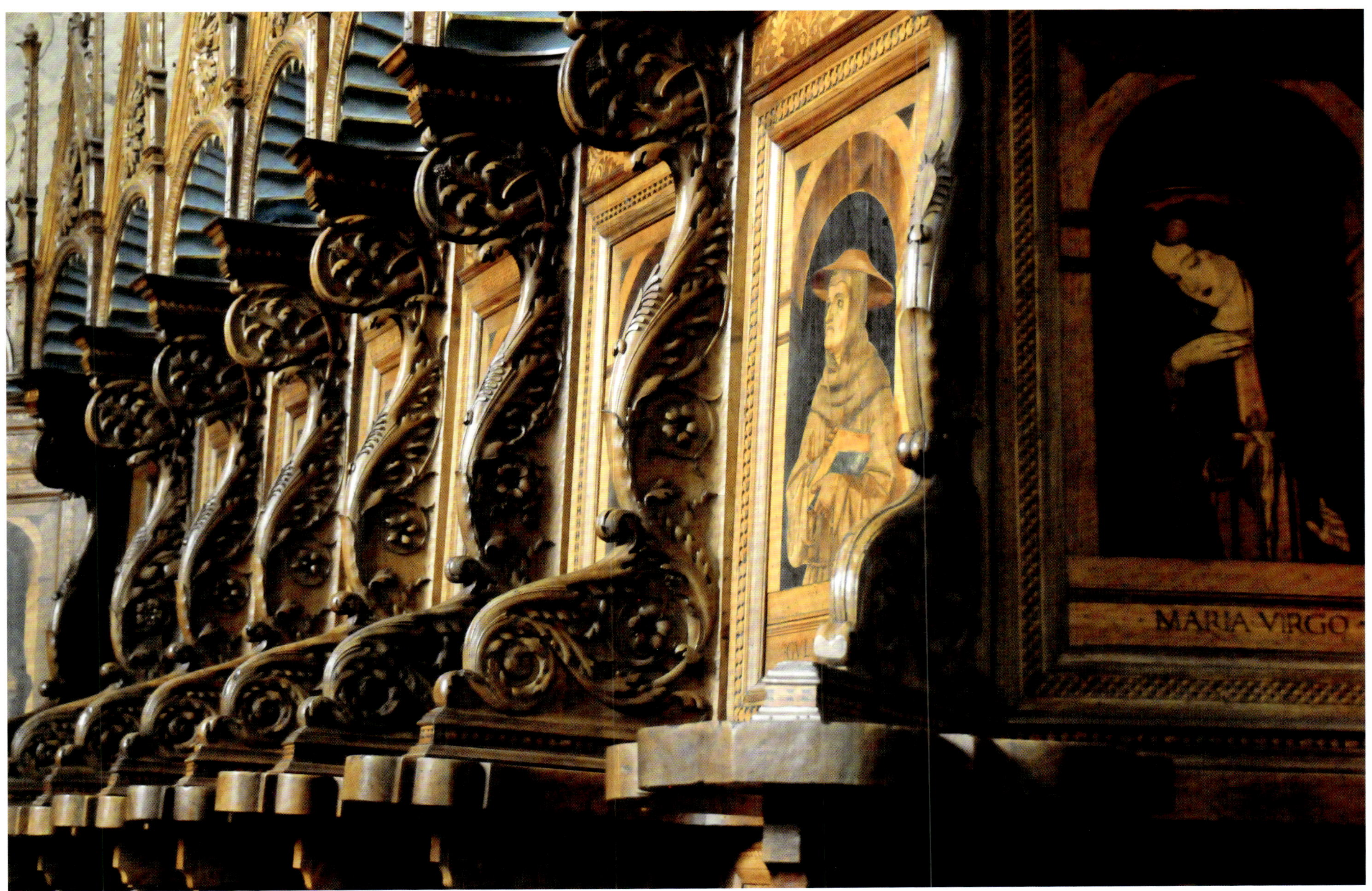
MARIA VIRGO

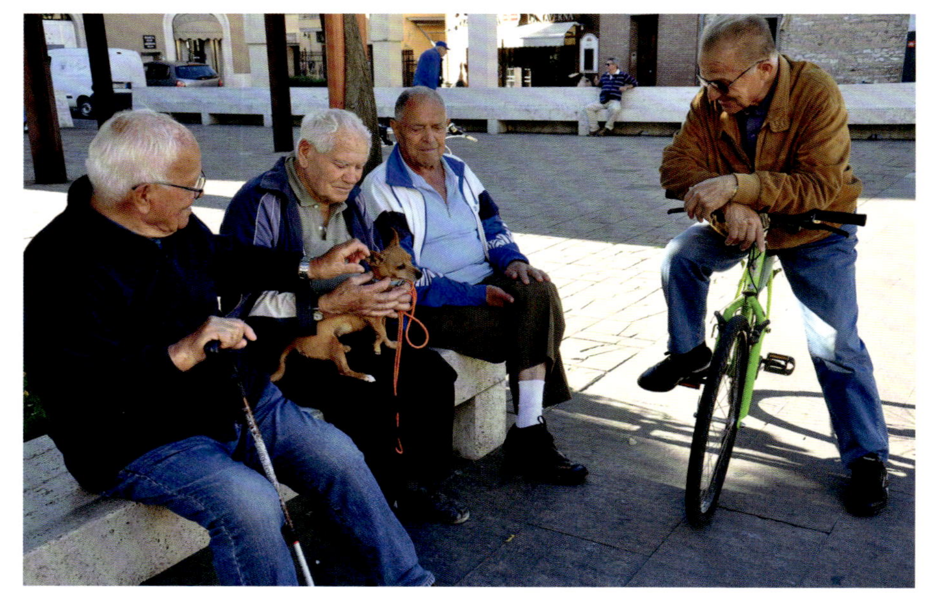

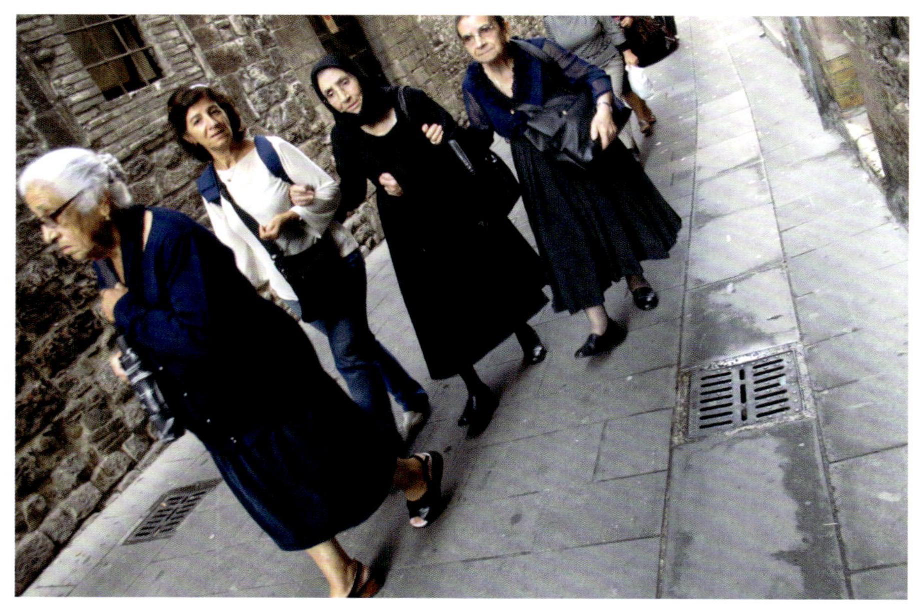

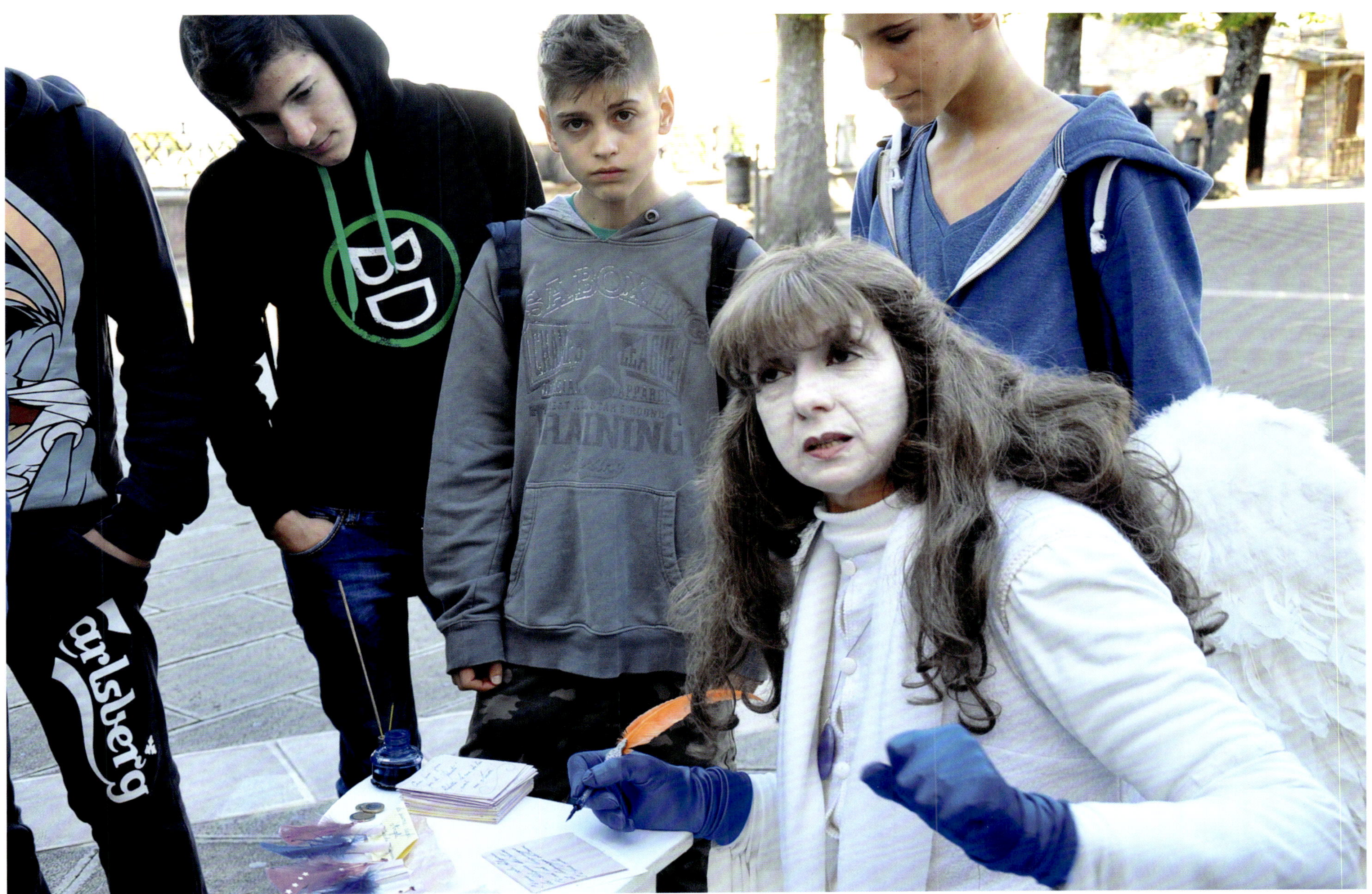
BD

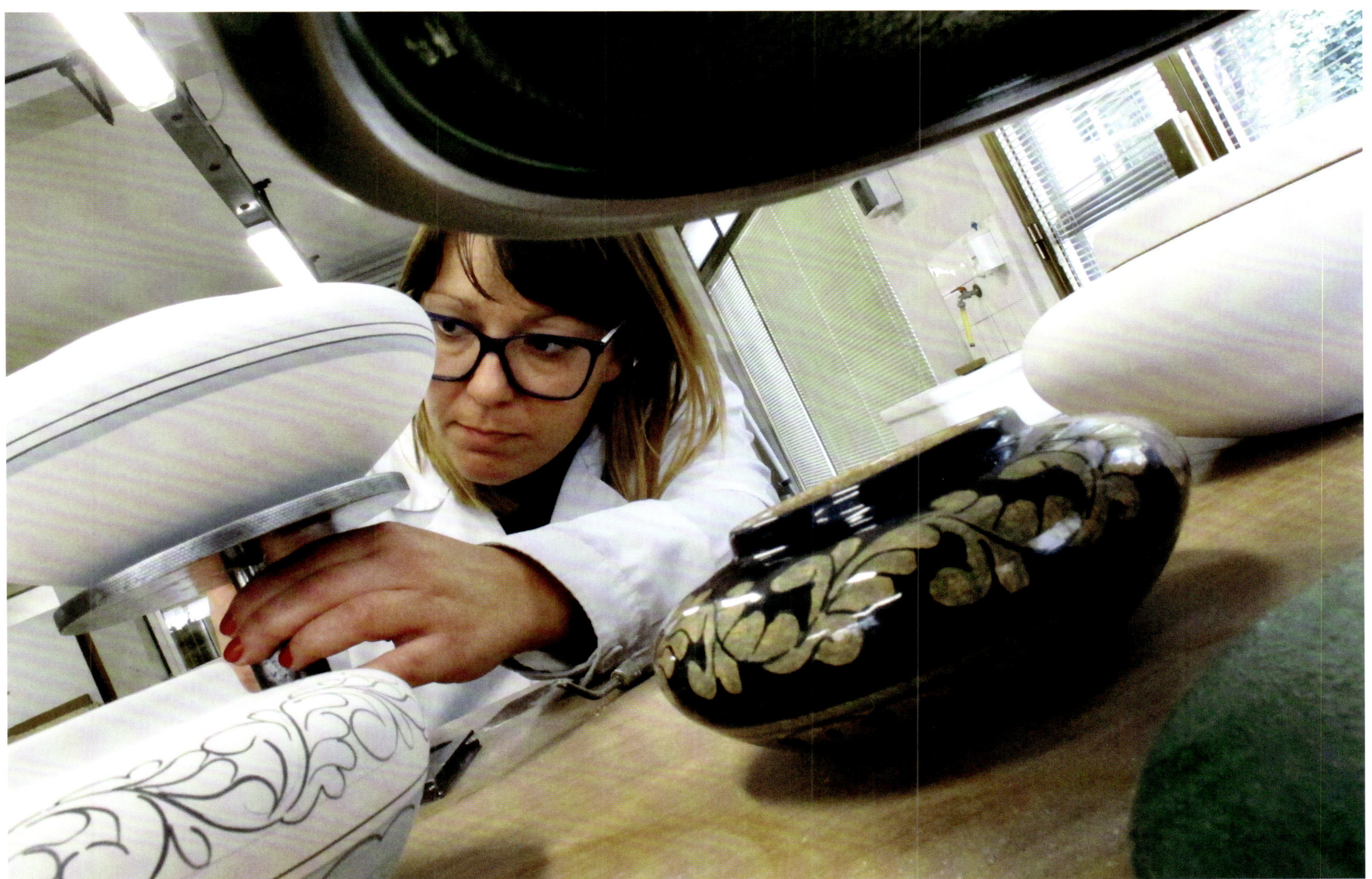

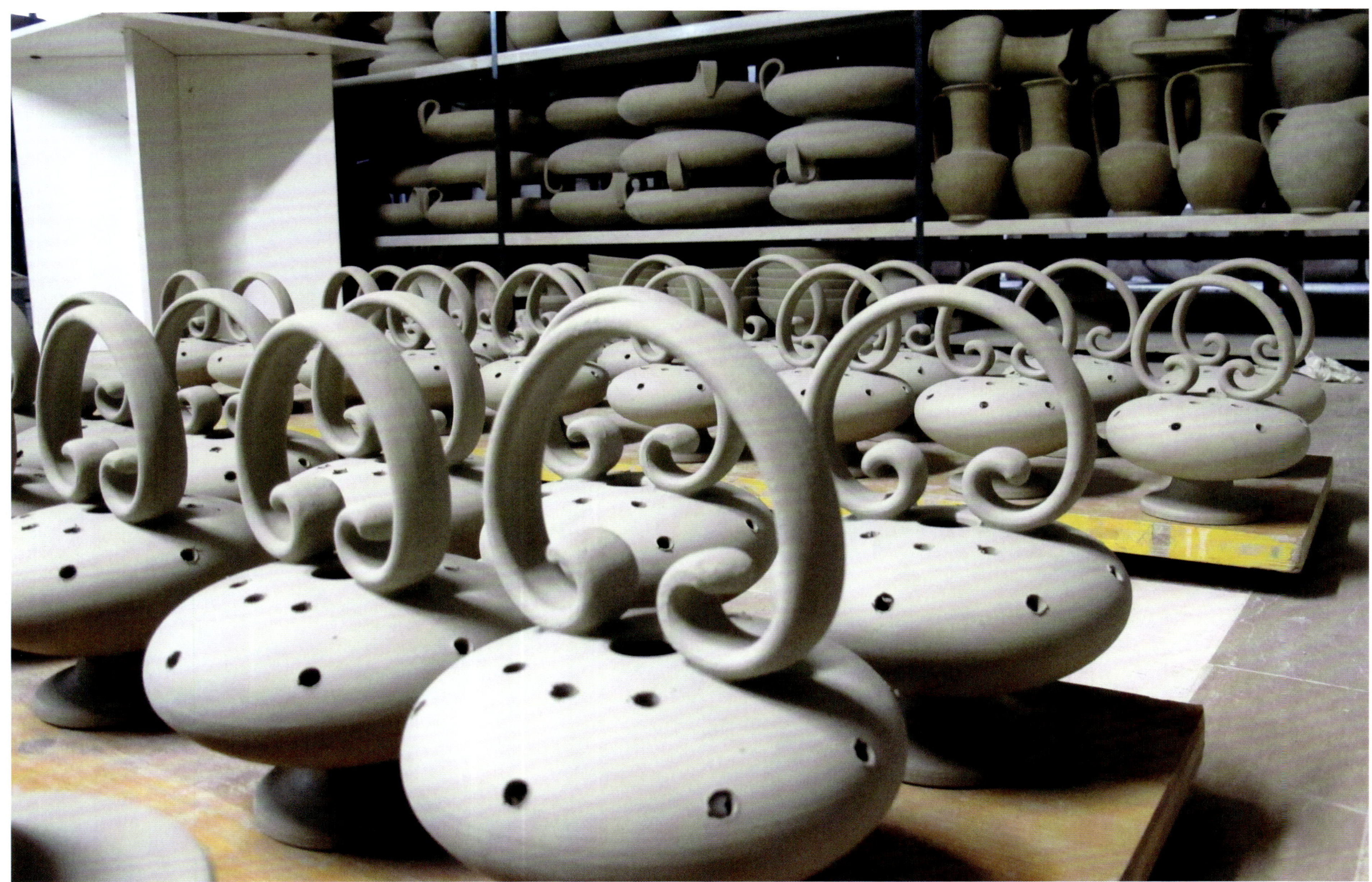

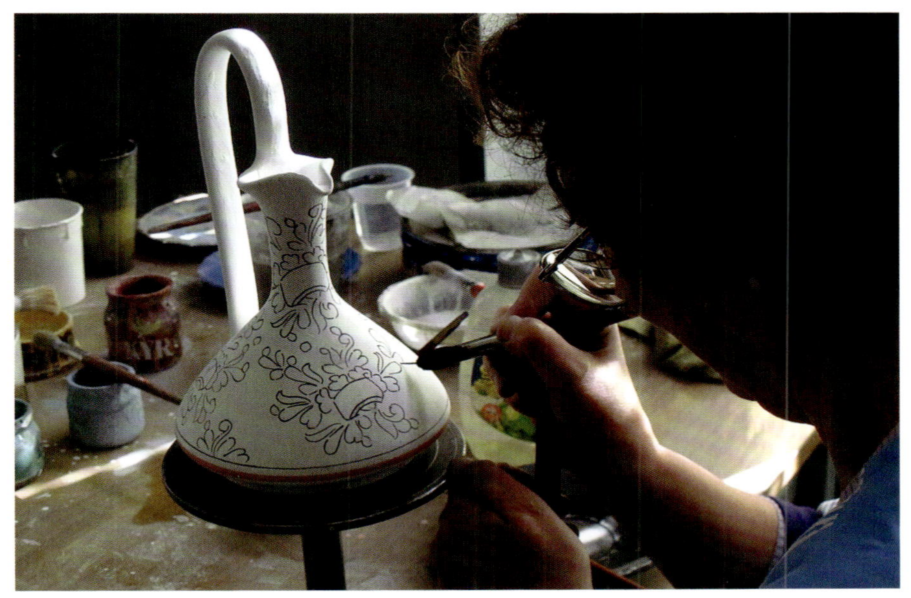

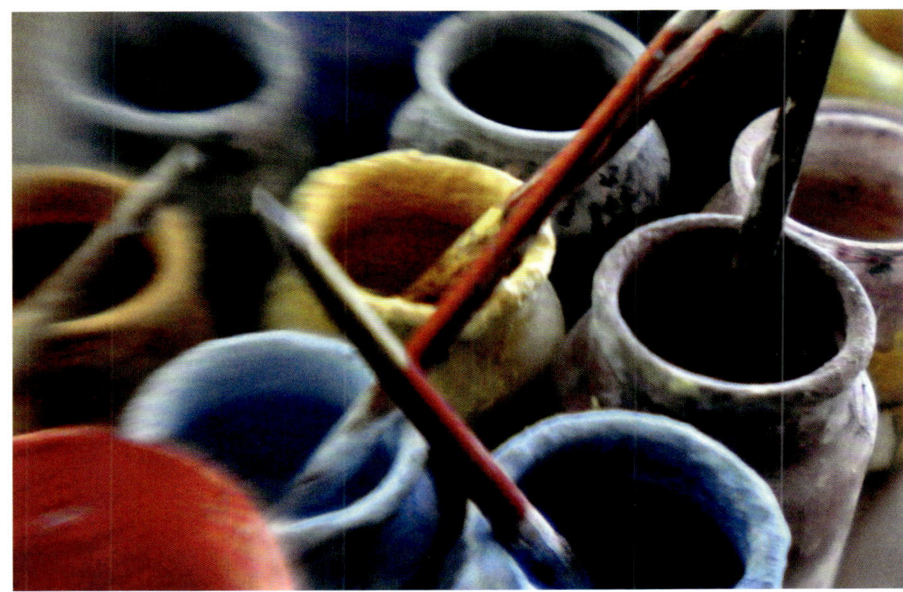

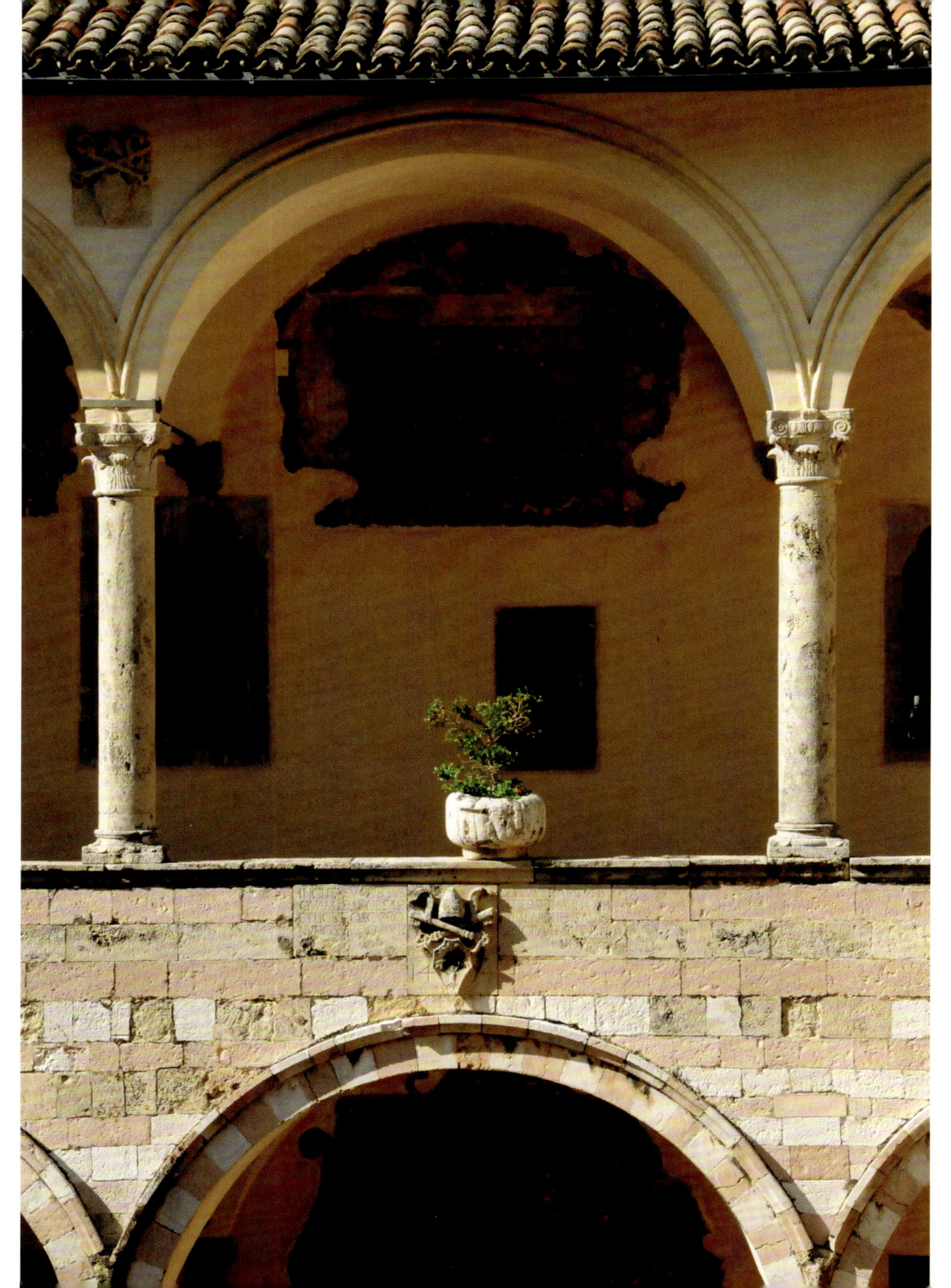

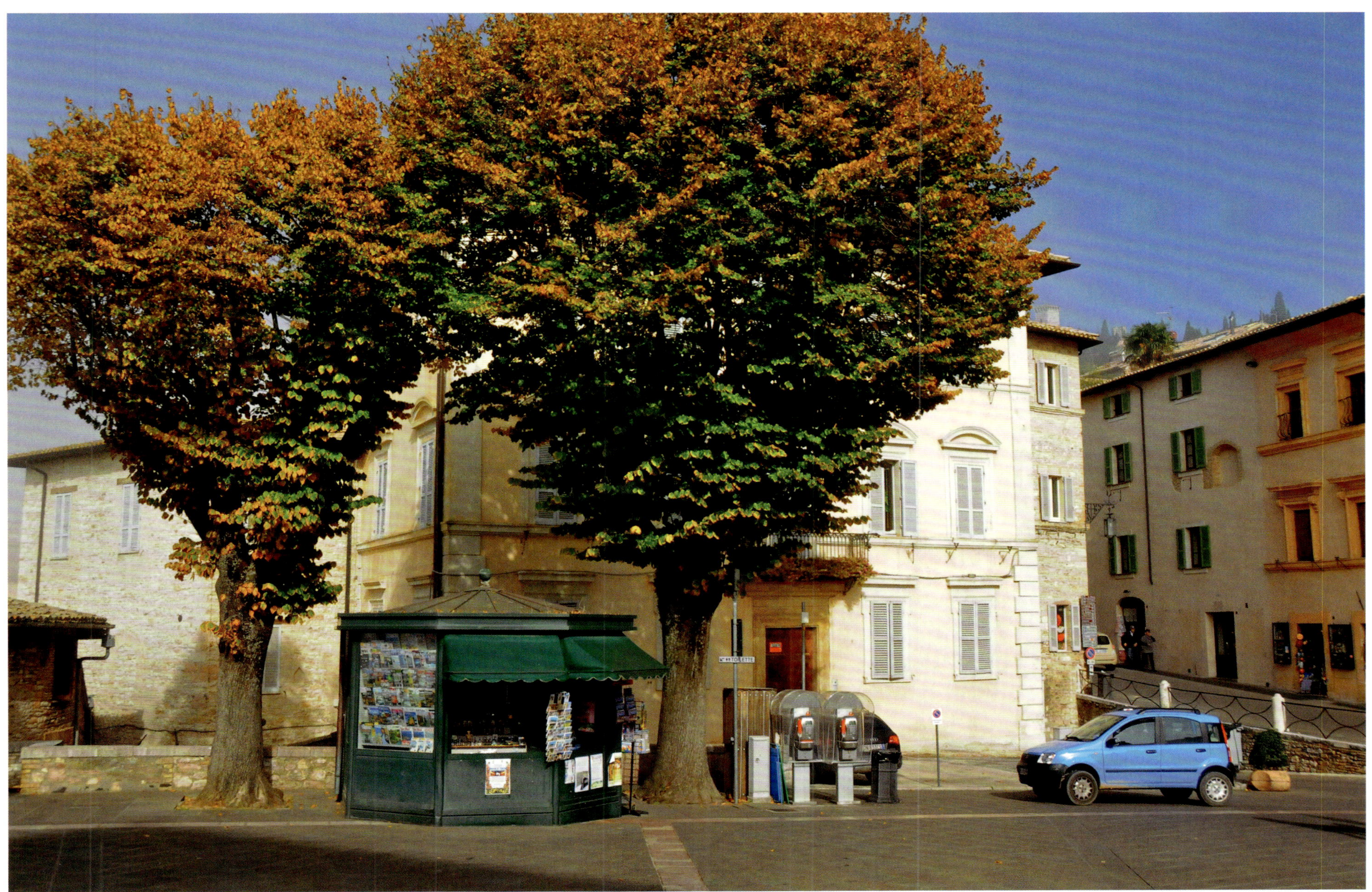

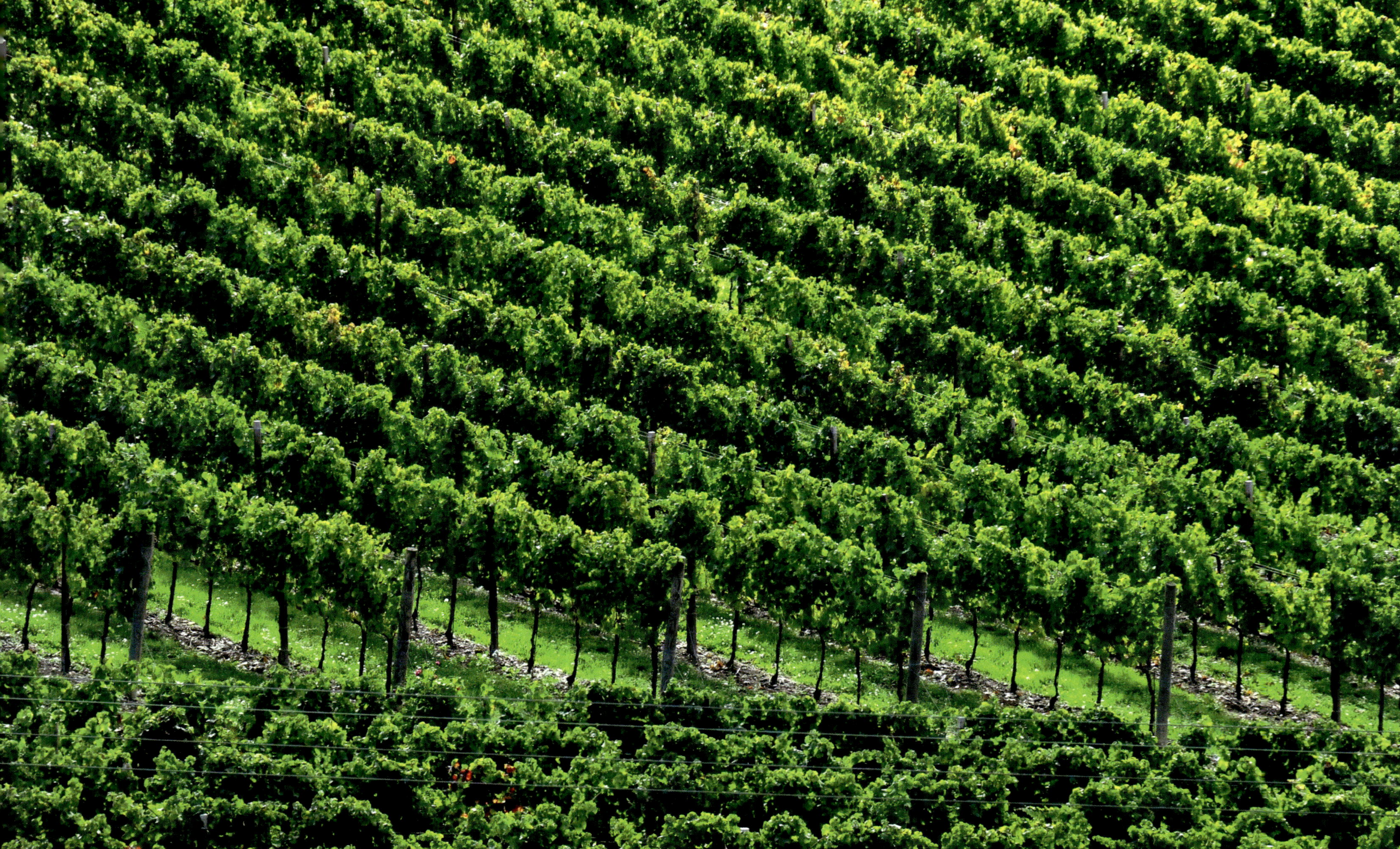

Montefalco

Named for its high hills and for the falcons that fly above it, Montefalco's spectacular views from its highest point also earn it the sobriquet, "The Balcony of Umbria." As with so many of Umbria's hill towns, its central square is a busy meeting place, ringed with cafes and shops, and peopled quite often with bicyclists in colorful spandex and cleats after a vigorous rally. Near the outskirts, beyond the town's outer wall, are acres of vineyards where Sagrantino grapes produce some of Italy's and the world's finest red wines. Some of the best are produced by Pardi vineyards, a venerable family-run business that also encompasses Tessitura Pardi, a small textile factory that produces woven linens of astounding intricacy in a clattering, crowded workplace.

Seeking Sagrantino: My Love Affair with the Best Italian Wine No One Knows

I first drank Sagrantino—Umbria's royalty of red wines—from a gas pump.

In 2010 Judy and I were nervously leading our first international photo workshop, based at a restored villa/*agriturismo* near the Umbrian town of Cannara, and one of our duties was to help prepare the villa for our six *studenti*. The owners of the villa, obviously hoping we would make this a regular thing (we did) gave us free use of the house and grounds that year, so we were more than willing to arrive a day or two early and help make it ready.

To ease our way (my Italian back then was middling), the villa owners called on Frances, their Italian-speaking American friend who lived in Rome. She happened to be staying at the villa during our week and—*miracolo!*—could meet us when we deplaned at Fiumicino and drive us the three hours to Cannara and to the Villa Fattoria del Gelso.

I should note that, though I was a seasoned traveler and journalist, the bulk of my professional flying experience involved White House and presidential campaign press charters (and one national book tour) where every logistical thing is taken care of—and your employer or publisher foots the (very big) bill. Being told that we would not have to worry about anything between Rome and the villa was like winning the lottery.

But it got even better.

As soon as Frances pulled up at the international arrivals terminal in her Fiat, I realized that we knew each other from the 1984 Mondale presidential campaign. Frances had been working press advance then and everyone knew her for her efficiency, as well as for her Texas accent.

Once we squeezed into Frances's tiny car, Judy's and my anxiety about our first international photo workshop lessened exponentially, especially since Frances's Italian was fluent, albeit with a certain twang.

Still, there were chores to do, and one of them over the ensuing days was to stock up on the red and white wine that our photo group would drink at the villa during the upcoming workshop week.

The Umbrian winery was large and beautiful, with an elegant tasting room. Bill and Suzy, the Americans who owned the villa, already had made the arrangements, and a personable fellow was more than happy to fill our four huge glass jugs with what I assumed would be drinkable red and white *vini di tavola*. He used a vinous gas pump, shooting cataracts of wine into our jugs using two separate nozzles, one for red, one for white, identical to the ones that we used back home in Washington, DC, to gas up our Volvo.

Given this humble background I was not prepared for my first taste of the red when we returned to the villa. "What is this!?" I exclaimed to Frances after my first sip. "Sagrantino," she replied. And so I came to know the finest wine in Umbria, and one of the best in all of Italy.

Rarely had I tasted a wine with such richness, depth, and complexity—especially in an ostensible jug wine. It may not have been the best wine I ever had tasted, but it came damn close, exceeded only by two French Bordeaux I had sampled many years earlier in the States. (During a press preview for the then-annual Heublein Premier Wine Auction, I sampled a 1952 Lafite Rothschild and a 1929 Calon-Segur, each of which nearly blew my head off.)

Sagrantino's history in Umbria goes way back, at least to the sixteenth century and possibly even to the time of the Roman philosopher-scholar Pliny the Elder more than a thousand years earlier. It is grown primarily in a small area in and around the Umbrian town of Montefalco, where it reigns as a varietal wine and also as a slightly less regal blend, combined with more common wines like Sangiovese.

Sagrantino not only is delicious—complex and assertive with strong notes of spice, dried cherry, and plum—it also is beautiful to look at in the glass: more dark purple than deep red. So popular were earlier versions of the wine that it had been used as a sacramental or communion wine, sometimes called "Sacrantino." It has one of the highest tannin levels of any wine in the world, giving it not only great flavor but also extraordinary capacity for bottle aging.

Interestingly, this also makes Sagrantino grapes perfect for a dessert wine, Passito, that is produced from thousands of grapes laid out on straw mats in the winery to slowly air dry and concentrate their sugars.

Can you blame me for being smitten?

And it was everywhere in Umbria. From large vineyard estates like Colsanto, to tiny family-run operations like Dionigi, Sagrantino was treated like wine royalty, carefully cultivated and bottled on site. At Montefalco—in effect, Sagrantino's ground zero—our workshop classes would look forward every year to a lavishly prepared Italian lunch served at Pardi vineyards, where each course was served with a different glorious red. We'd start with blends, then graduate at the roasted meat course to their glorious DOCG Sagrantino.

If Sagrantino exploded my universe of red wines, Grechetto, one of Umbria's most famous white wines, also was a revelation, if not quite so dramatic. After all, I already loved Orvieto, the dry Italian white wine named after one of Umbria's loveliest cities. What I did not know was that this wine is largely composed of Grechetto grapes. It was only after staying in Umbria that I enjoyed Grechetto as a stand-alone varietal wine and marveled at its crisp dryness—in stunning contrast, say, to some California chardonnays, that seem to coat the tongue with an oily, almost cloying, presence. (Like Sagrantino, Grechetto grapes also can produce a superb vin santo dessert wine.)

All that remained after our first Umbria workshop was to rebook the villa for the following year—and to find these great wines at home.

Great on the first; not so great on the second.

For years after our first visit to Umbria, I'd ask for Sagrantino at my favorite shops in Washington and be met with blank stares. Grechetto, too. But, happily, that is changing. Still, it is almost impossible to find any selection among Sagrantinos or Grechettos in DC, so I oftentimes find myself simply grabbing any that I can find. Happily, neither seems to be wildly overpriced—yet.

Ironically, I *was* able to have my pick of Sagrantinos in, of all places, the tiny former fishing village of Lubec, Maine, where we had a summer home for nearly forty years.

One summer, as we enjoyed lunch on the deck of the town's best restaurant, The Water Street Tavern and Inn, owner Jim Heyer joined us as the lunch rush ended. On a whim, I asked Jim, who is a wine aficionado, whether he ever had heard of a wine called Sagrantino. He had not. "I'll be right back," he said, and went to fetch the printed list of wines from his wholesaler.

Sure enough, the wholesaler listed not one, but three different Sagrantinos, of different prices. "Which one should I order?" Jim asked. I picked the one in the middle: Colpetrone Montefalco Sagrantino. And now, whenever we sit down to dinner at Jim's restaurant, an open bottle of the wine, breathing nicely, is waiting for us.

But I only can dream of the gas-pump Sagrantino we enjoyed near Cannara on that first trip to Umbria. In later years we saw that gas-pump wine, at least for commercially available table wine, was not uncommon. Once, touring a huge Umbrian supermarket where we knew the manager, we were amazed to see—besides whole prosciuttos hanging on a rack for the taking—an elegant selection of premium wines, including Sagrantino, that was worthy of the best wine shops in Manhattan or Washington.

But what caught Judy's and my eye was the room off to the side where sat what only could be viewed as a gas pump, with nozzles on either side—one for red wine; one for white—for customers to use. That experience called to mind a trip Judy and I made to Provence in the early '80s visiting our friends Neil and Carol Offen, two American writers then living in the snug little hill town of Bonnieux in the Luberon. They, too, knew the joys of gas-pump vino.

"I remember we used a five-liter jerry can," Neil said, "and that we had choices between red and white, and then among differing alcohol levels (12%, 13, maybe 13.5 or 14). Like you in Umbria, we filled the can through a hose, holding the gas gauge trigger. The five liters cost around ten or twelve francs, meaning a standard bottle (.75 of a liter) cost more or less a franc a bottle, or at that time, about forty-five cents. Yes, not only cheaper than gas, but cheaper than water."

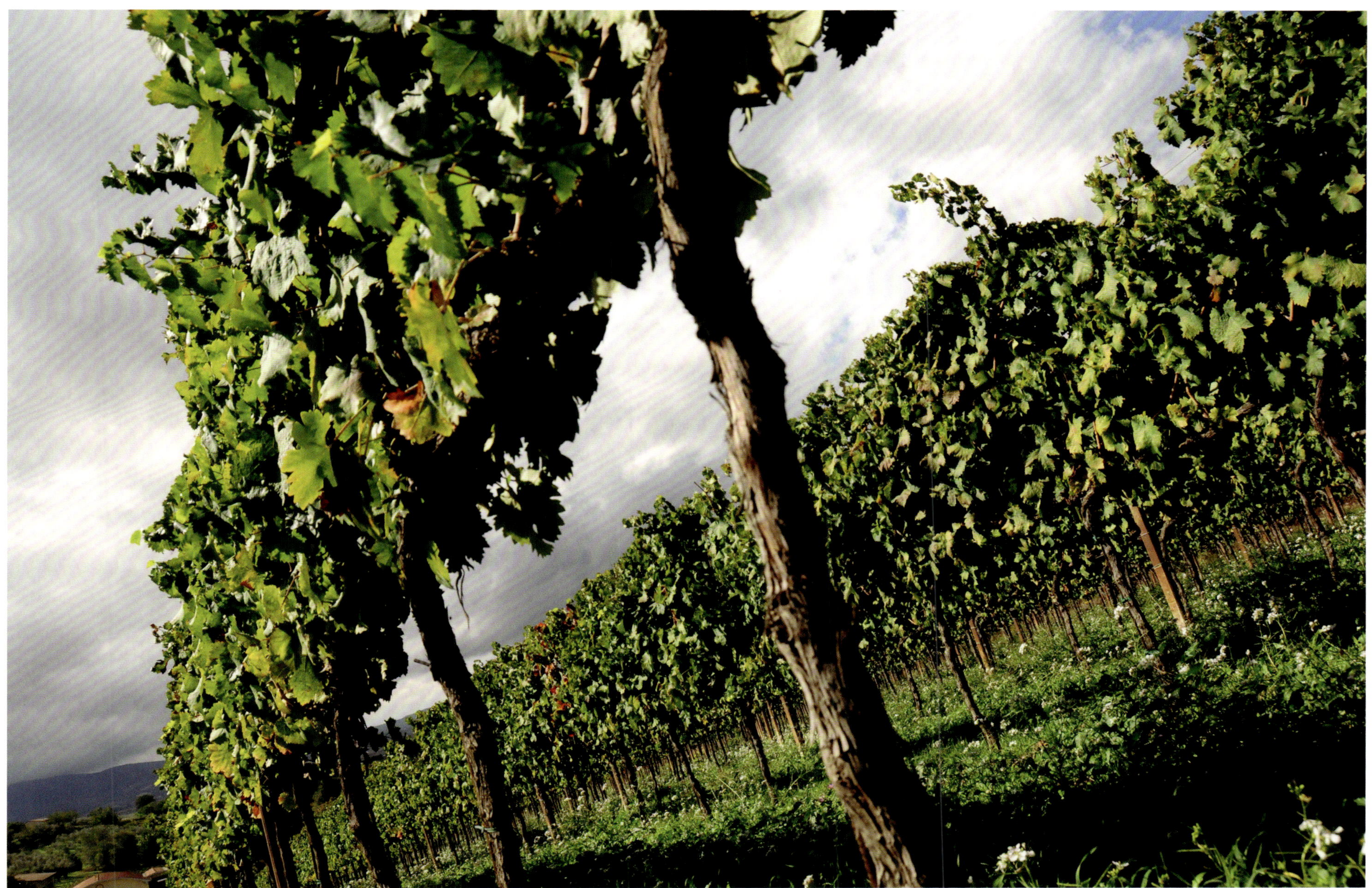

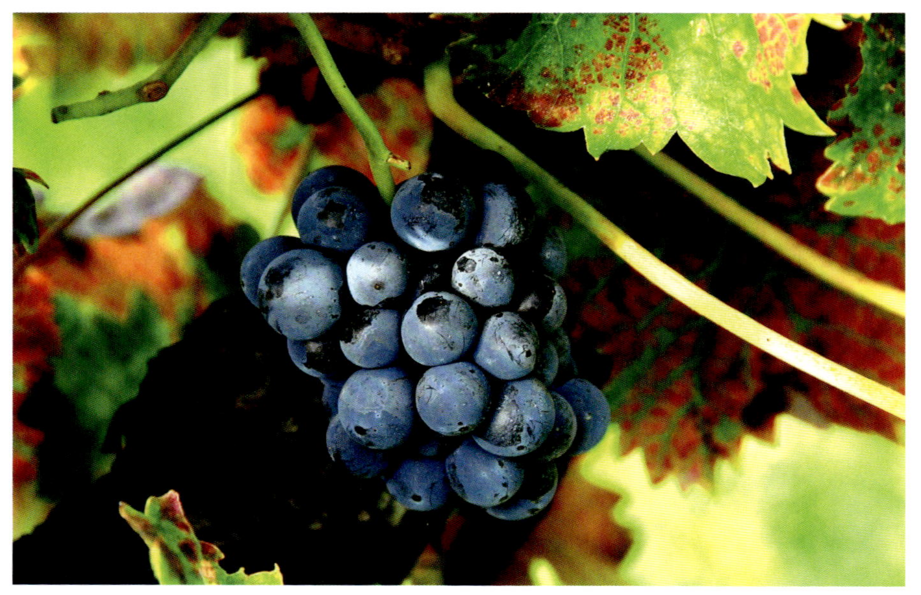

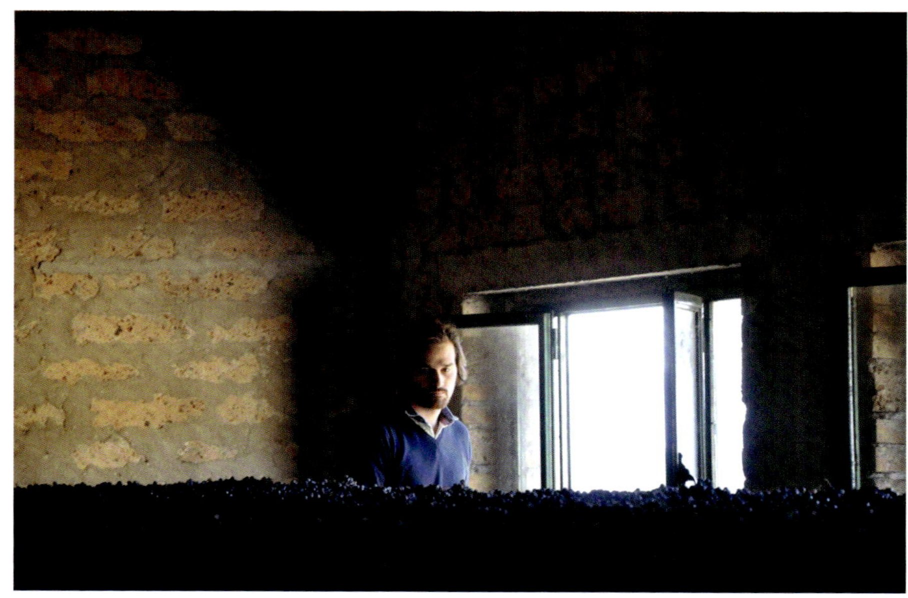

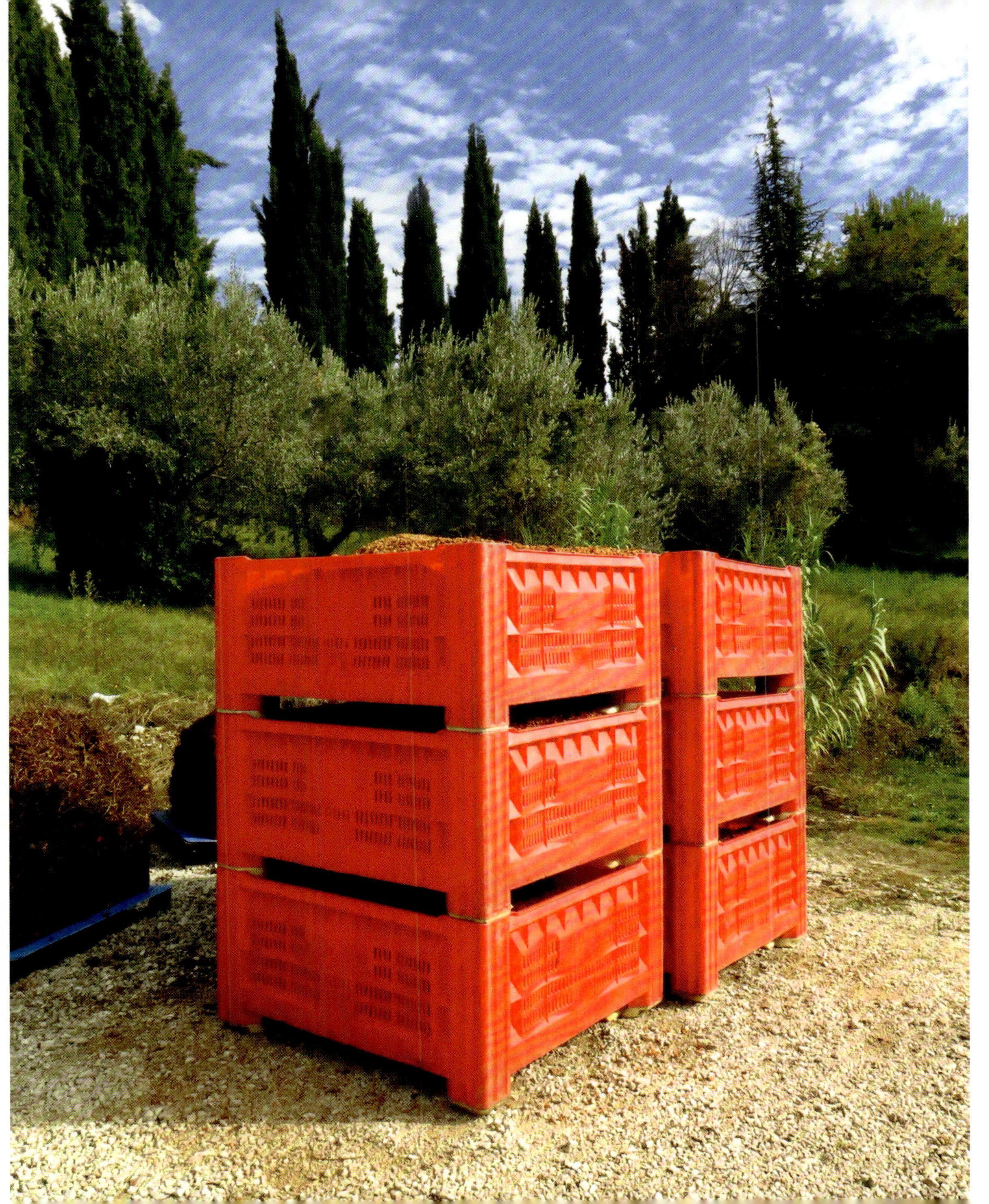

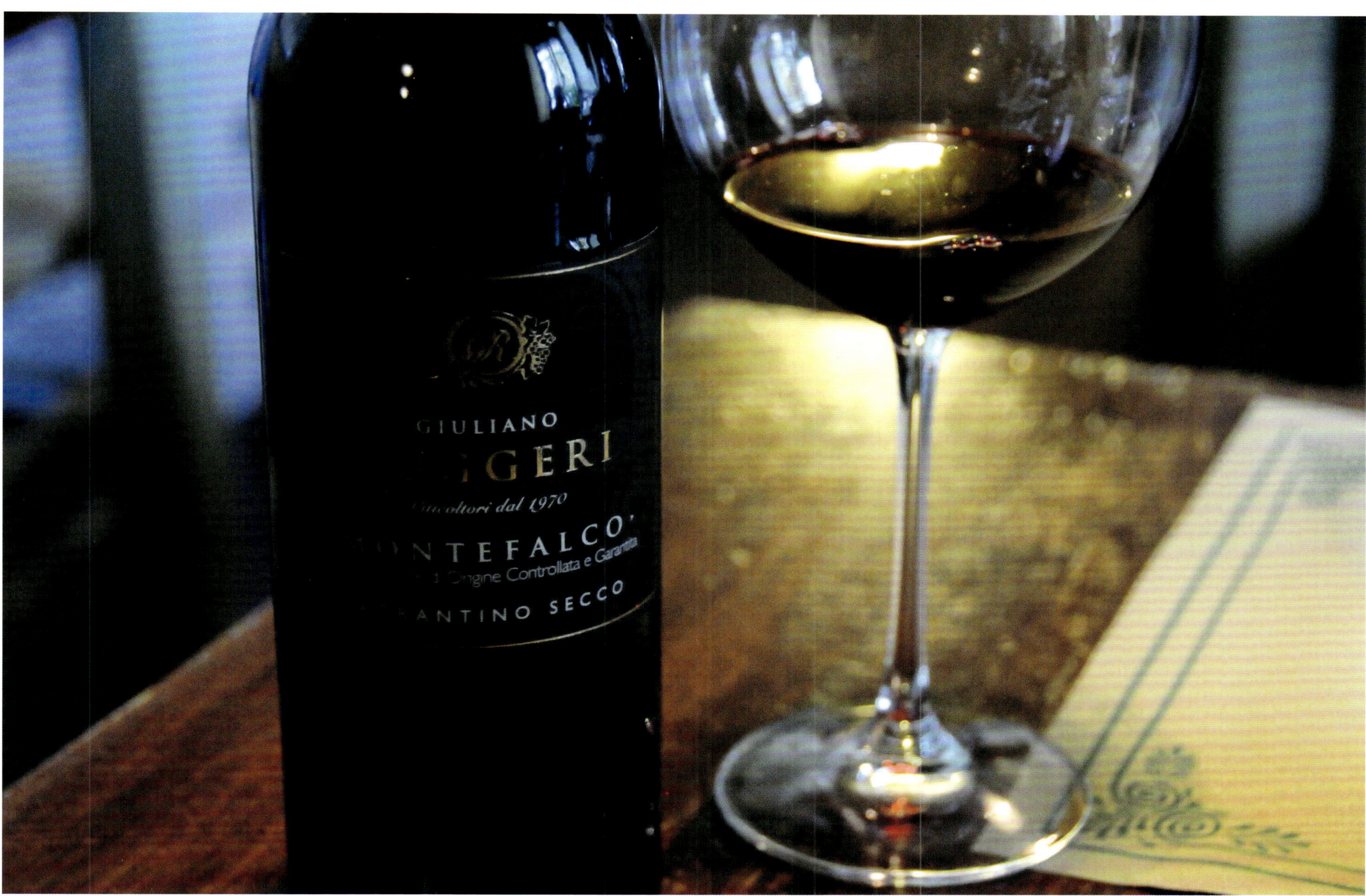
GIULIANO
Origine Controllata e Garantita
SECCO

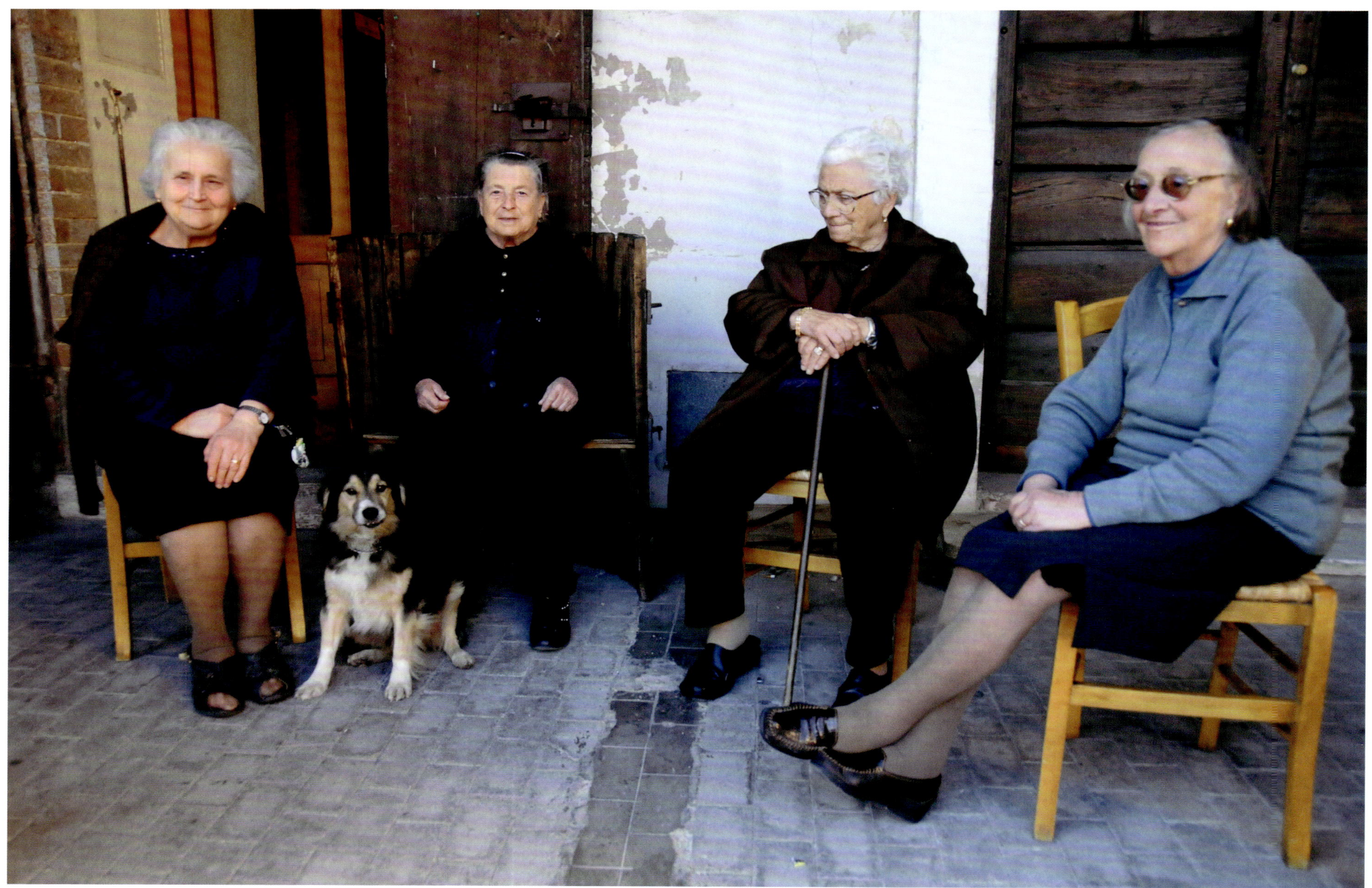

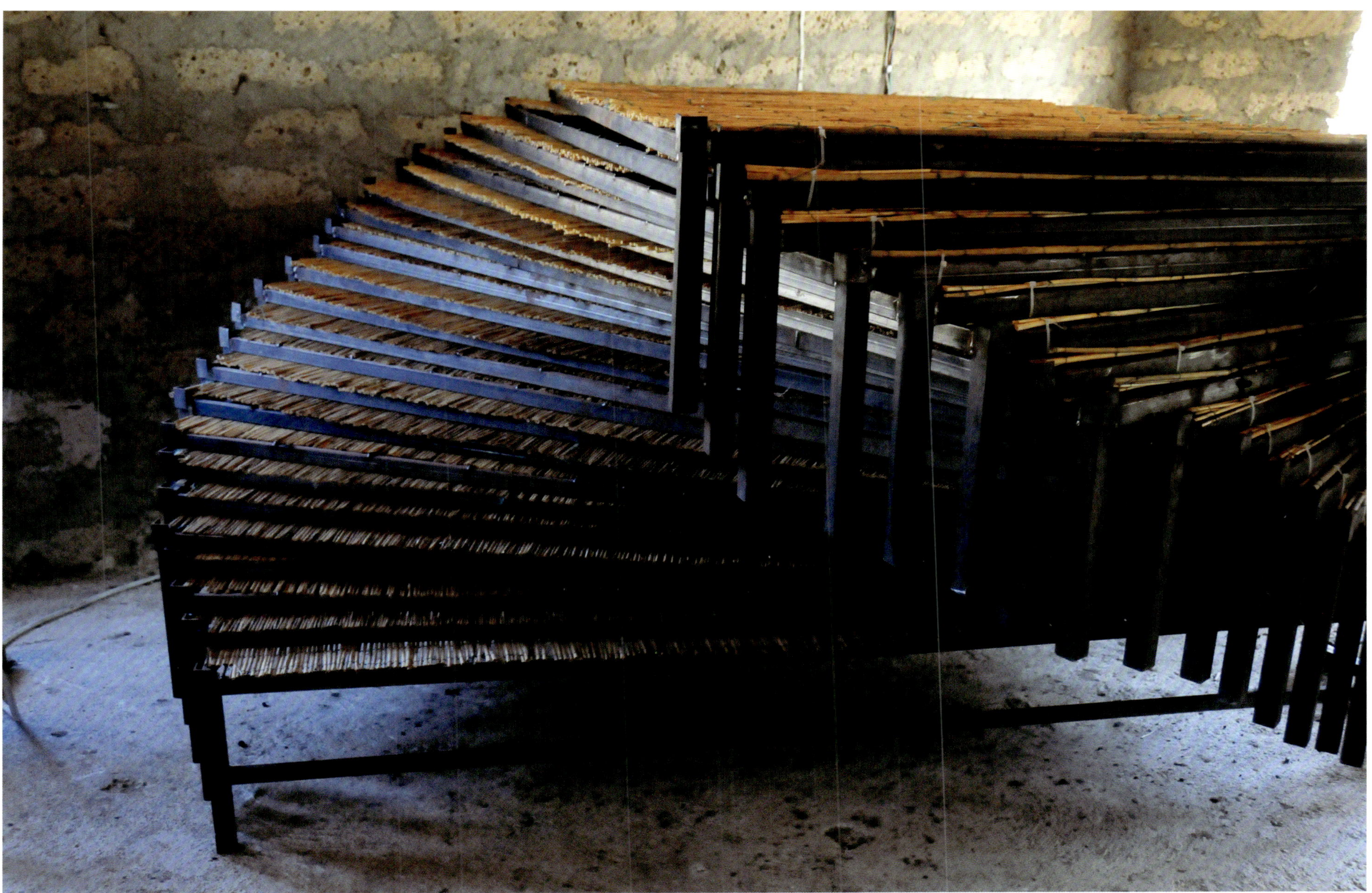

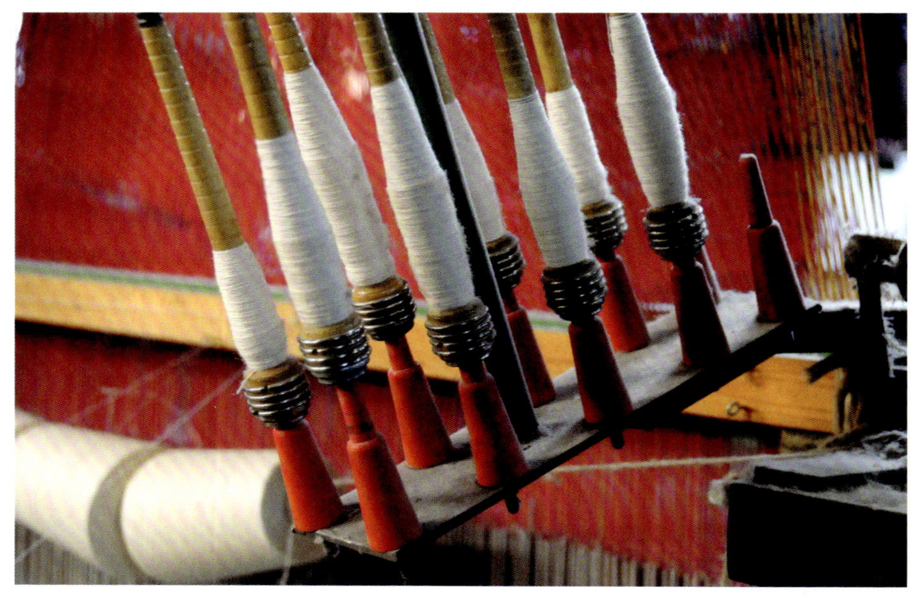

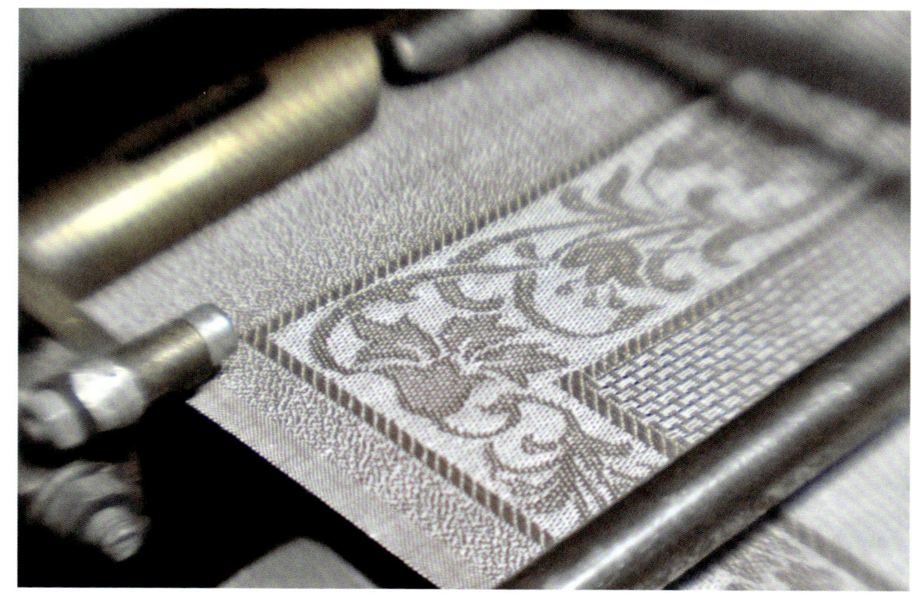

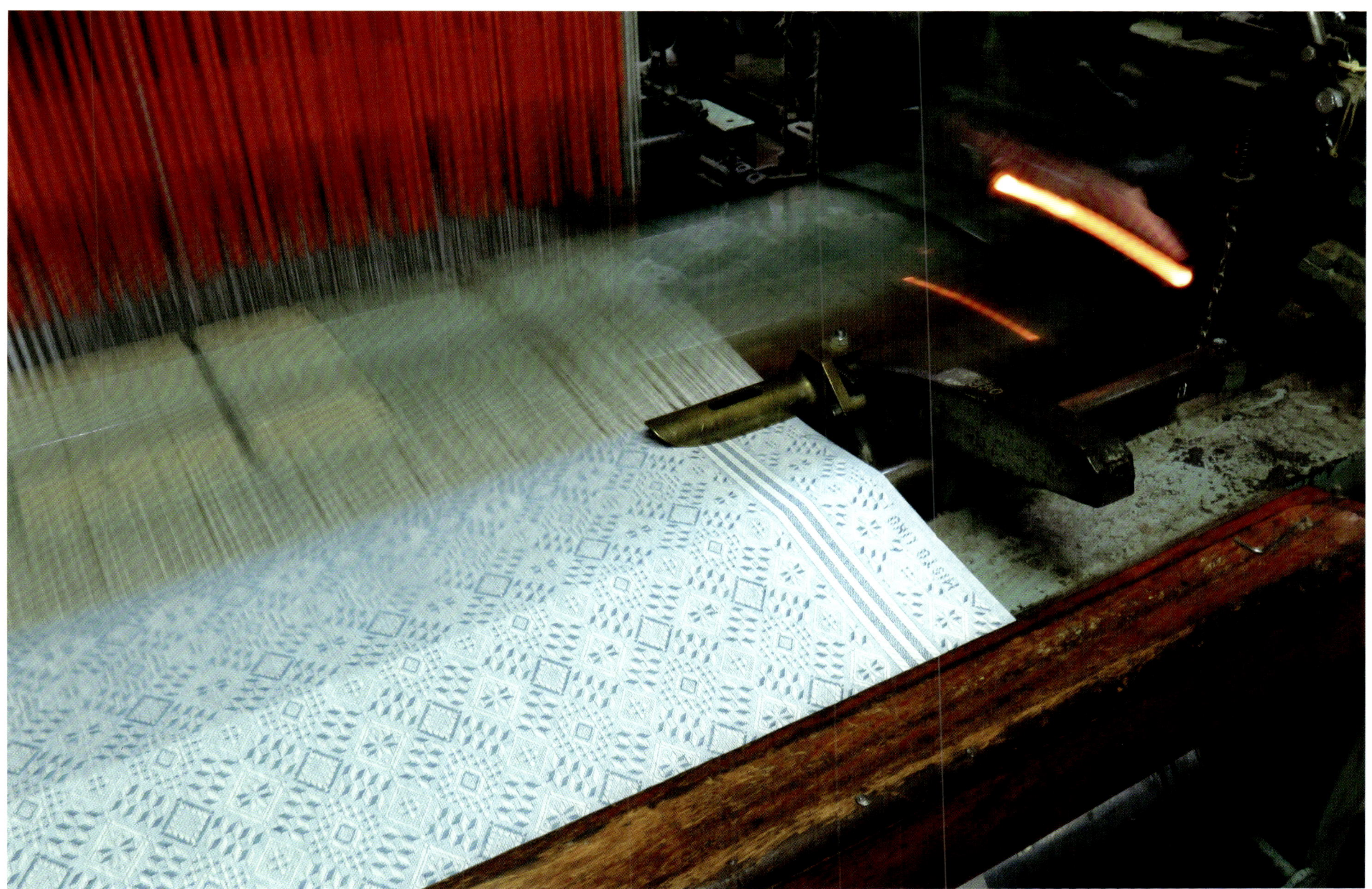

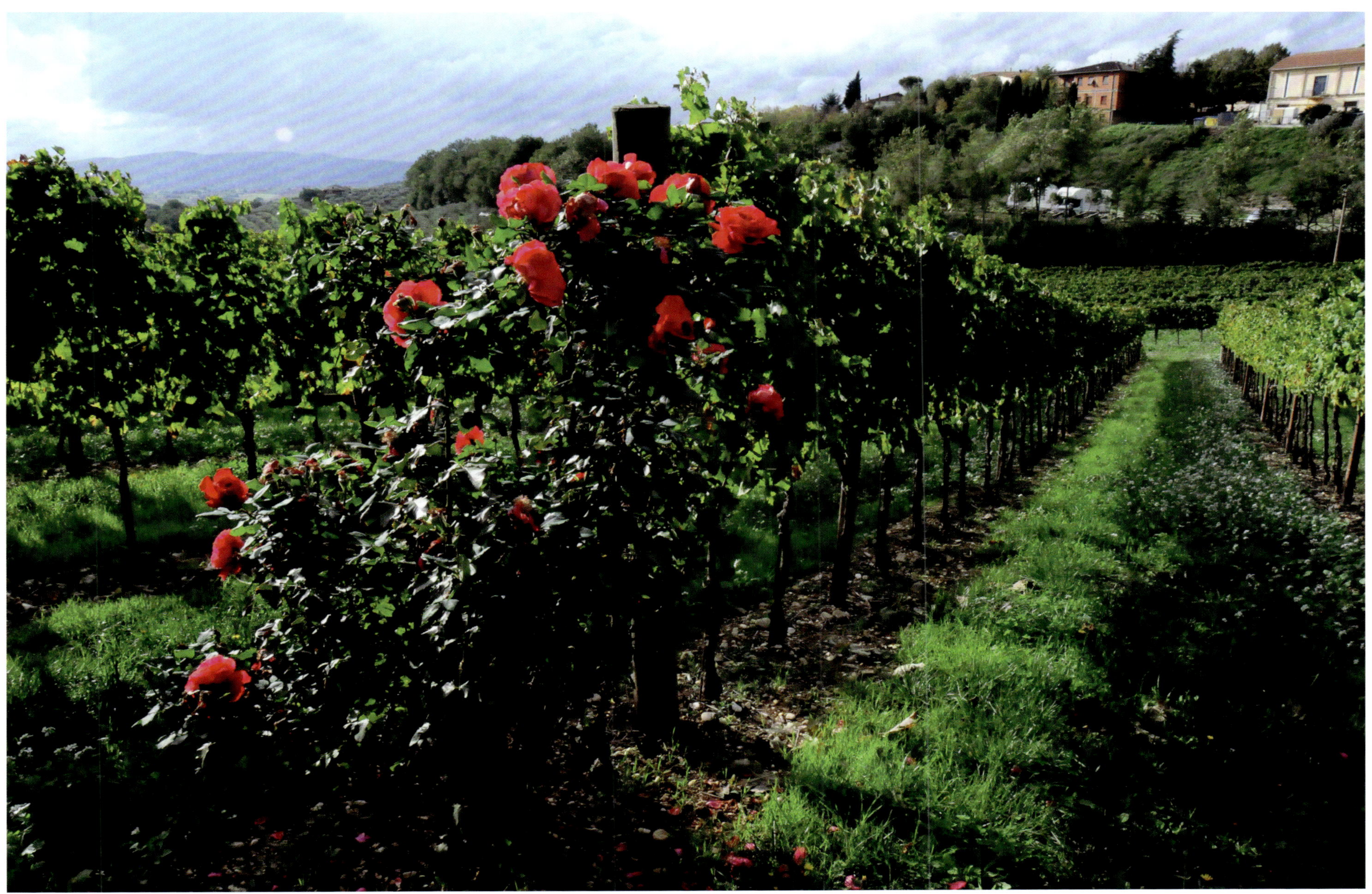

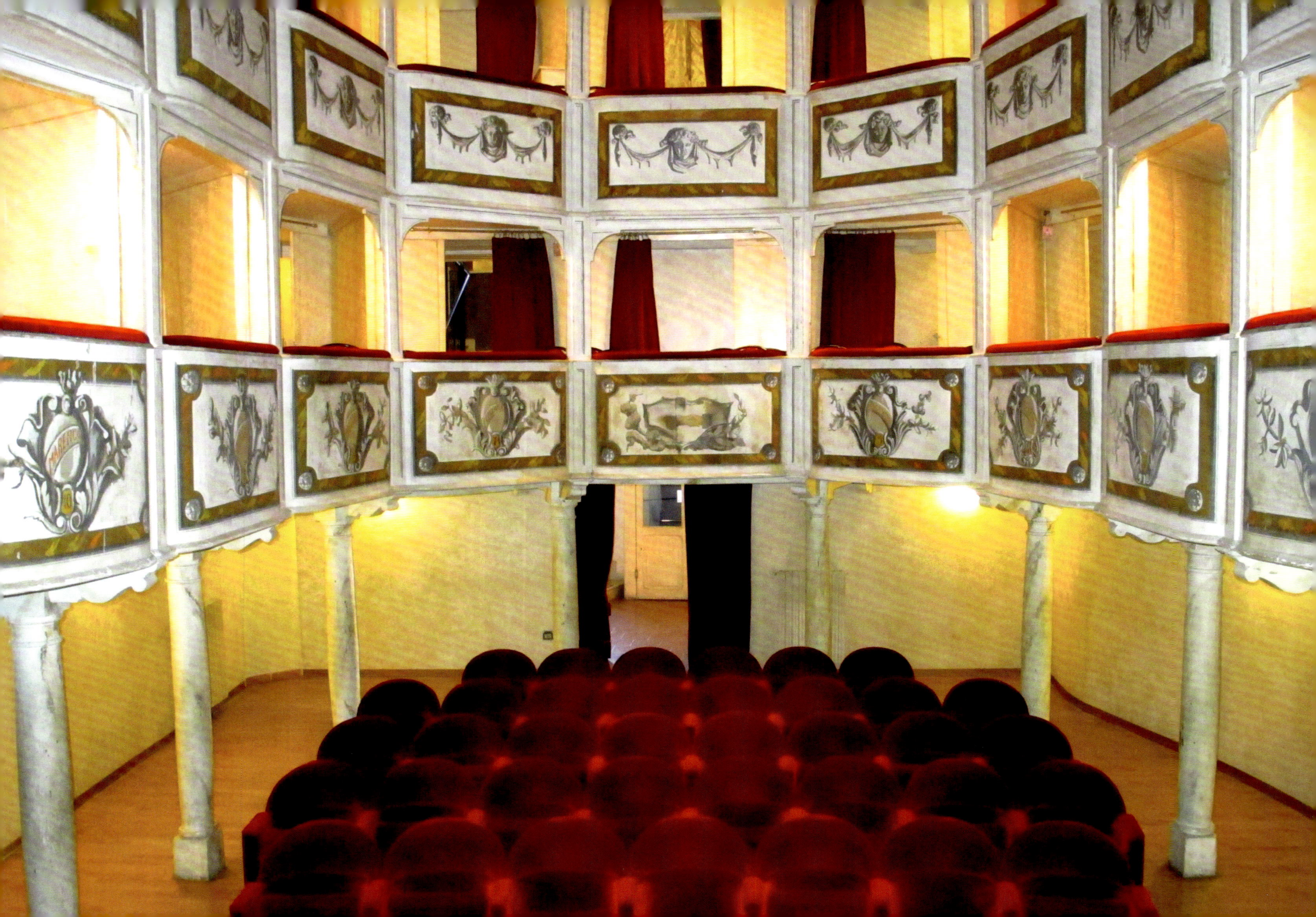

Monte Castello di Vibio

Listen closely at the top of this tiny town and you will hear only the wind. Even normal everyday bustle is muted here because of the town's small size, which tends to discourage all but the most determined tour buses. But that also highlights its most noted attraction, the Teatro della Concordia, literally the world's smallest opera house, with but ninety-nine seats. Decades ago, the town's citizens saved the opera house from destruction, voting to increase their taxes to finance its restoration. Money well spent. It now attracts tourists in proportion to its size while having secured its place in Italy's cultural history.

The Smallest Opera House

At the highest point in the tiny Umbrian hill town of Monte Castello di Vibio sits an equally tiny gem of a theater, the Teatro della Concordia. Lovingly preserved and open to all, it is the smallest opera house in the world, with all of ninety-nine seats.

As a boy, I remember listening to opera, broadcast live on the radio from the Met in New York City every Saturday, as my mother, the former Carmela Casullo, vacuumed our walk-up apartment in the Bronx. The soaring voices and dramatic music easily overpowered the Electrolux as slowly, inexorably, I formed a lasting bond with this touchstone of Italian culture.

Decades later, as I stood for the first time in the elegant confines of the Teatro della Concordia, those feelings surfaced again as recorded arias played while my wife, Judy, and I walked through what seemed like a miniature world of gilt, trompe l'oeil, and red velvet.

The theater was built at the beginning of the nineteenth century and opened in 1808, during the Napoleonic Wars. Nine wealthy Umbrian families financed the theater to reflect and support the cultural ideals of freedom, equality, and brotherhood (hence "Concordia") that went beyond the goals of the French Revolution.

Immediately, the theater was a point of pride in the small hill town, though it took decades for its tiny interior to be decorated with trompe l'oeil paintings, first by artist Cesare Agretti, and later by his son Luigi, who, amazingly, began working on the theater's bell-shaped ceiling (cherubs, nymphs, birds, flowers), heraldic shields on the stalls (touting Italian greats like Dante and Goldoni), a painted backdrop depicting the town of Monte Castello di Vibio, and a captivating and whimsical treatment of the walls of the upper-floor lobby making the room look as if it were hung with tent-like tapestry—complete with a pussycat peering in over the folds.

Claiming the mantle of smallest opera house, or smallest theater, in the world was not without controversy. There are far smaller performance spaces all over, and not just in Europe. However, only Teatro della Concordia is a faithful reproduction, but on a much smaller scale, of much grander European and Italian theaters. It has a classic bell-shaped floor plan, proscenium stage, dressing rooms, and ticket booth—even a grand staircase entrance at the front of its building. In short, Teatro della Concordia arguably is everything that La Scala is in Milan, or La Fenice in Venice, but in miniature.

My parents were far from rich (it was a Bronx walk-up, remember), but Mom made sure to set aside money every year for her nosebleed tickets to the Metropolitan Opera, especially after it moved to its luxurious new home at Lincoln Center in 1966. On the rare times I accompanied my parents, I was in good company: some 3,800 opera lovers filled the huge Metropolitan Opera House.

It was a similarly overwhelming feeling decades later when Judy and I enjoyed a sold-out performance of *Cosi Fan Tutti* at the Kennedy Center opera house in Washington. We were joined by nearly 2,400 other opera lovers at this temple to the arts on the Potomac.

How different it is in Monte Castello di Vibio. The whole town has only slightly more than 1,600 souls, meaning that the *entire population* of Monte Castello di Vibio could fill the Metropolitan Opera House, twice, with 600 seats to spare.

Even La Fenice in Venice, a restored space that I adore for its intimacy, not to mention its near-blinding opulence, can hold a thousand people. For years every January we would bring our Venice-in-Winter photo workshop groups there to photograph from Napoleon's box—and every year our students were overwhelmed by what they saw. This rare combination of intimacy and grandeur makes it feel as if you could wear the opera house around your shoulders, like an elegant scarf or stylish yet comfortable coat. The feeling is hard to imagine if you have not been there.

Imagine what that feeling of intimacy would be among Teatro della Concordia's mere ninety-nine seats: thirty-seven red velvet theater seats on the ground floor directly facing the stage; the remaining sixty-two high-backed chairs scattered among eighteen intimate boxes that ring the bell-shaped theater on two upper floors.

A wonderful photo from 1929 shows just how popular the little theater was. The grainy image shows a heck of a lot more than ninety-nine folks crowded onto the main floor and into the stalls for who knows what kind of performance back then. You cannot look at this photo without flashing back to the wonderful crowd scenes in the 1988 film *Cinema Paradiso*.

All manner of entertainments have taken place in the Teatro. In 1945, an eighteen-year-old unknown named Gina Lollobrigida played in the Eduardo Scarpetta comedy *Santarellina*, one of the first public appearances in a career that would see Lollobrigida become an international film star, a respected photojournalist, philanthropist, and 2008 lifetime achievement awardee from the National Italian American Foundation.

Though it survived the World War II years intact, the theater closed in 1951 and fell into neglect. In the 1960s, the stalls collapsed, and it appeared that Teatro della Concordia would go the way of the fictional Cinema Paradiso. In fact, there was a plan to raze the building and create an open town square in its location. Happily, that scheme foundered after townspeople agreed to pay extra taxes to help begin needed restoration of the historic building. In 1981, the town formally purchased the theater and restored it under the direction of architects Paolo Leonelli and Mario Struzzi. (As fortune would have it, when construction was begun, it was discovered that the theater's existing wooden pillars were strong enough for the interior to be restored in its original form.)

Today the theater enjoys popularity in proportion to its tiny size. It regularly features concerts, recitals, and plays (and also can be rented for civil weddings). But in fact, the theater, not to mention the town of Monte Castello di Vibio, probably could not accommodate much more attention beyond a tour bus or two—and even that would be a stretch. (I did see one such bus in Todi, with a picture of the theater festooned on its side.)

Unlike Todi a half hour to the south and awash in amenities to complement its beauty, Monte Castello di Vibio does not even have in-town parking. You park at the base of the town and start walking. Since it is such a small place, the walk is not onerous, the well-kept stone houses and buildings are gorgeous, and the view from the top is splendid. Still, a horde of tourists wielding selfie sticks is perhaps the last thing Monte Castello di Vibio needs.

A nineteenth-century document, describing the Teatro's opening, noted that its creators "made it little so it would be proportionate with their town." With remarkable prescience, the document added that "civilization is not measured in volume or square footage."

Or, for that matter, in tourist traffic.

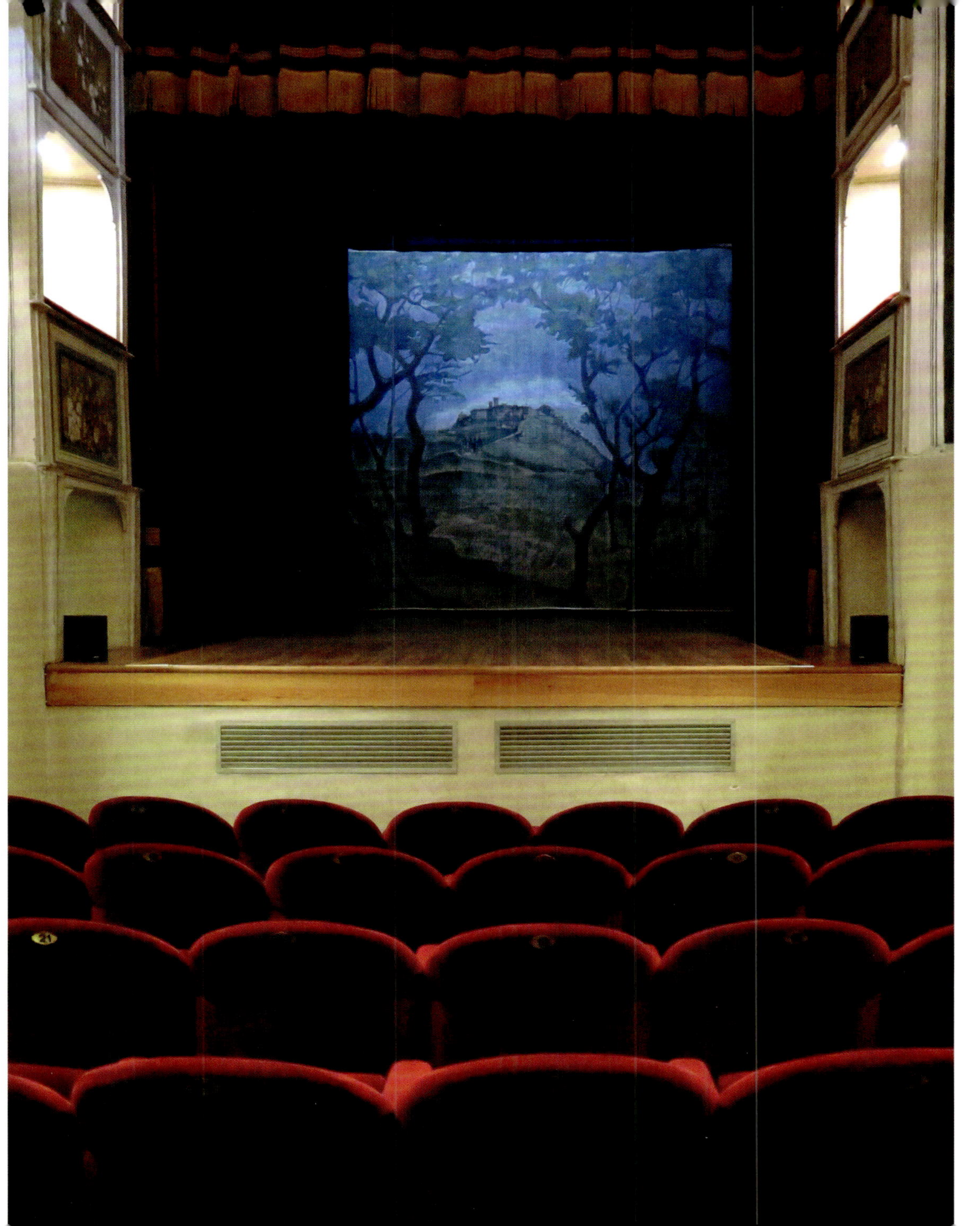

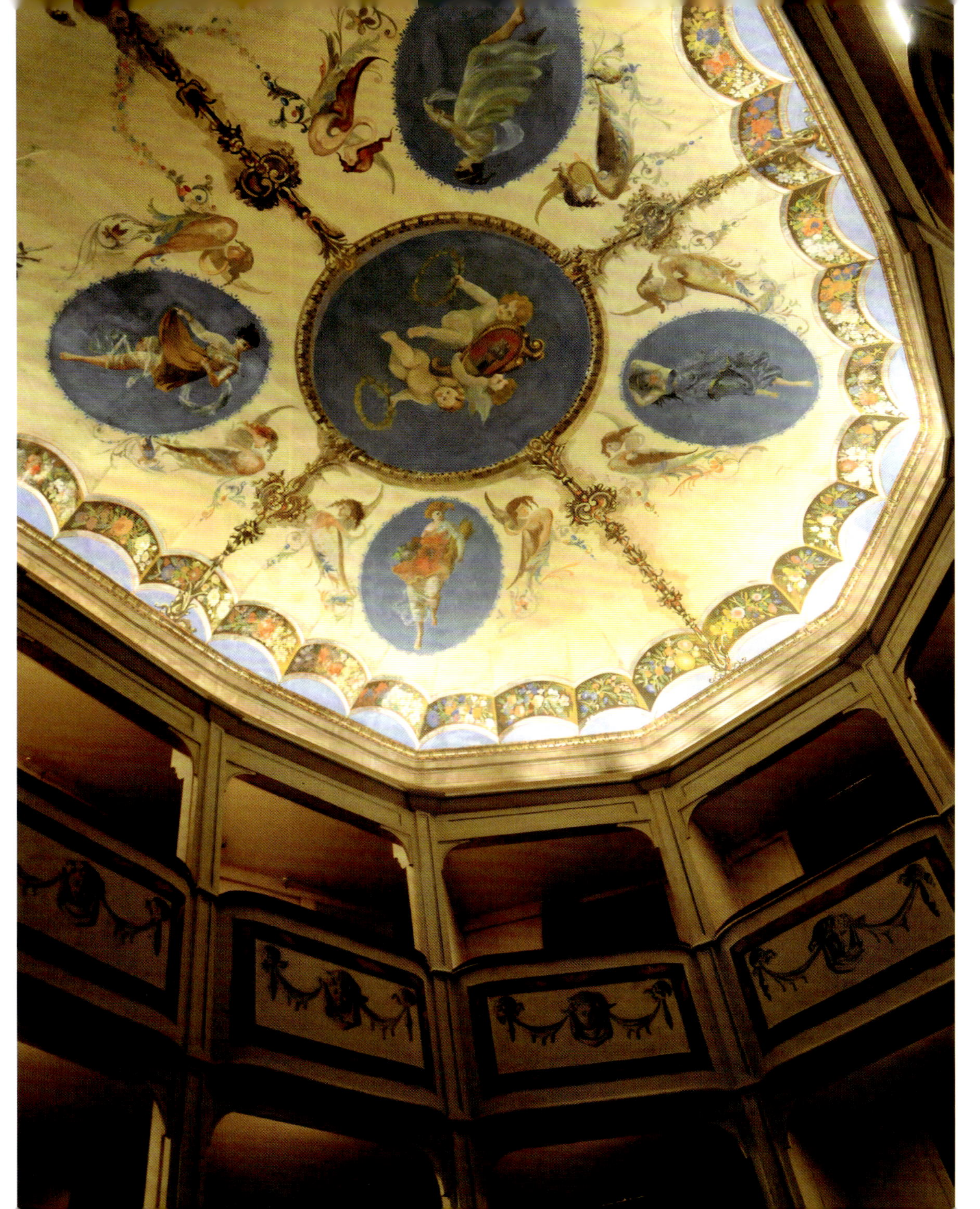

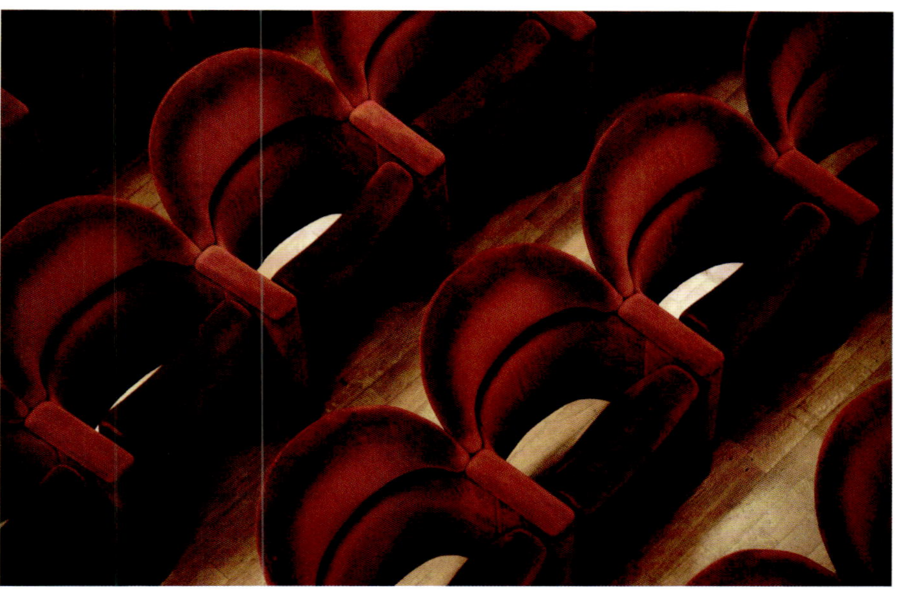

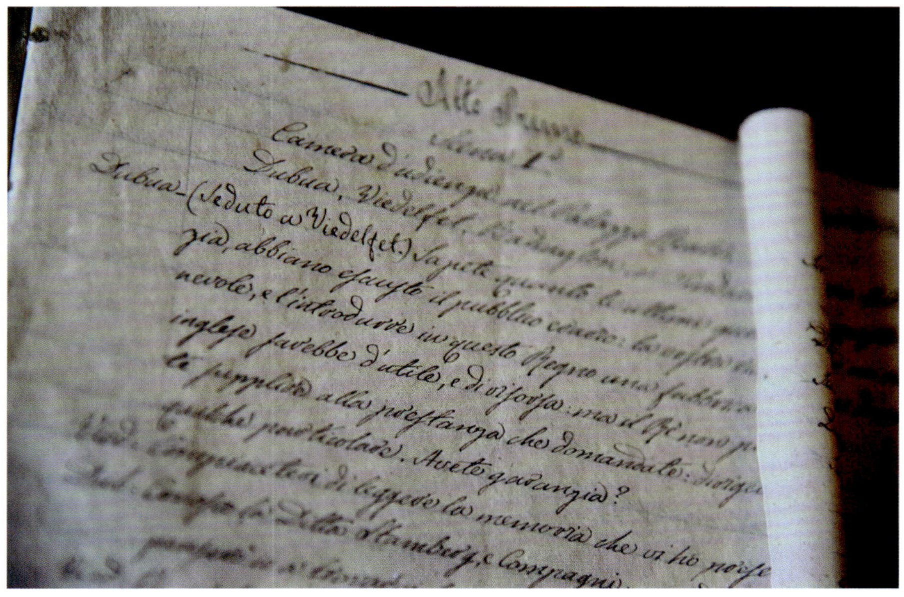

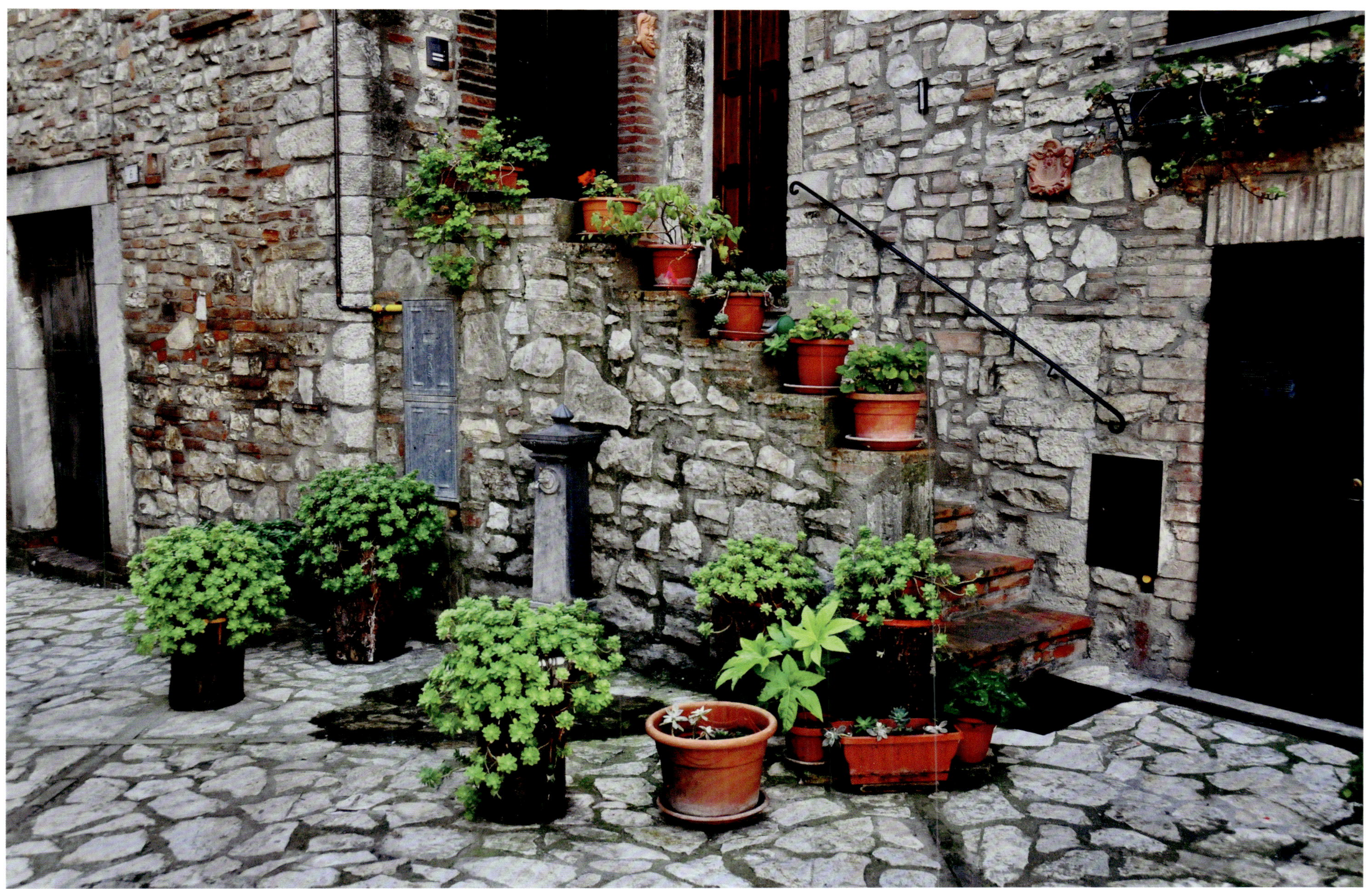

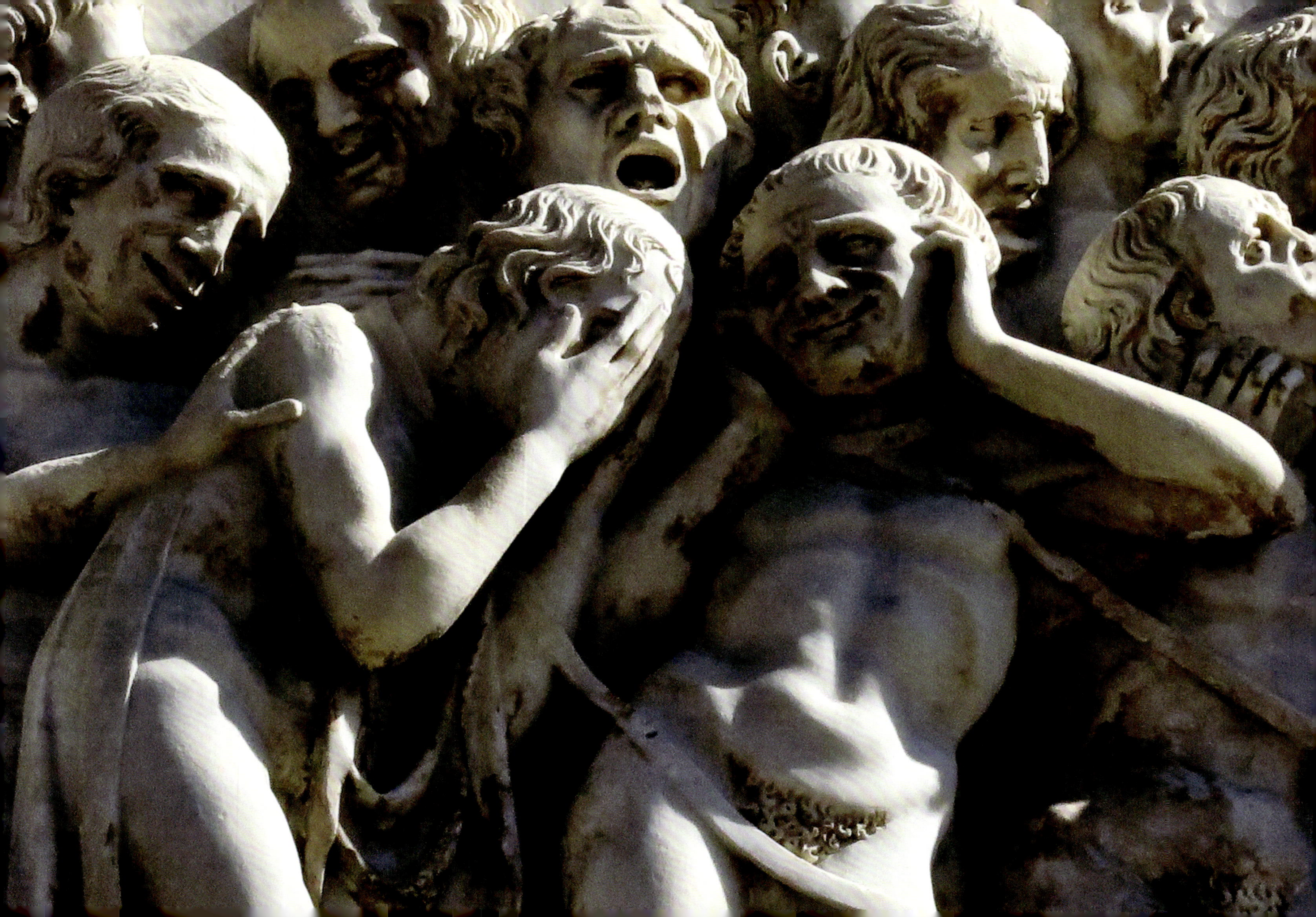

Orvieto

An elegant city (and a small one, to be sure, with 20,000-plus people, compared to Rome's more than 4 million), Orvieto charms most visitors with its combination of lovely old villas, public parks and monuments, walkable streets—and arguably the most austerely beautiful Catholic church in the world, La Cattedrale di Santa Maria Assunta, which took three centuries to build. Like Assisi, Orvieto attracts hordes of tourists, which obviously can be a mixed blessing, especially if you previously have warmed to the charms of similar places like Norcia, Bevagna, or Todi. But comparisons can be both helpful as well as invidious. After all, Orvieto at its most touristy is nothing like the Ginza in Tokyo on a warm spring night, London during the holidays—or New York City at any time at all.

Orvieto: The Most Beautiful Church in the World

St. Patrick's Cathedral in Manhattan is more ornate, and St. Peter's Basilica in Rome is more important ecclesiastically.

The papal basilica of St. Francis of Assisi may be more stunning artistically, and the Shrine of the Immaculate Conception in Washington, DC—with its Byzantine cupola inspiring off-color jibes about a tattooed breast—is certainly more over-the-top.

Don't even mention Antoni Gaudí's amazing church in Barcelona honoring La Sagrada Familia—literally the largest unfinished Catholic church in the world.

These magnificent houses of worship notwithstanding, for my money the most beautiful Catholic church I've ever seen is the quietly eloquent Duomo di Orvieto, la Cattedrale di Santa Maria Assunta, dedicated to the Assumption of the Virgin Mary into heaven. It sits atop the highest point in that small Umbrian city and challenges all comers not to marvel at how perfectly its different elements come together in grandeur and grace.

I first saw the Duomo di Orvieto more than a decade ago as my wife and I began our photography workshops in Umbria. Back then, I have to say, it was low on our list. Our earlier workshops leaned more toward the big-ticket tourist sites like Perugia and Assisi.

But, too often, our fall workshops coincided with events like Perugia's annual chocolate festival, when seemingly every chocoholic on the planet descends on Perugia in a cocoa haze, jamming its narrow streets, making it even more difficult to navigate, much less make good photographs.

And that was nothing compared to the crowds thronging Assisi's Basilica di San Francesco that time of year. Revered by pilgrims for his selflessness, gentleness, and asceticism, Francis generates big crowds in the church—not to mention all over town. Thousands go there annually to pray to the saint and to see masterpieces on the basilica's towering walls and entranceways by artists from Cimabue to Giotto.

I confess I might have put up with the huge Assisi crowds, including friars (?) roaming the streets dressed like St. Francis, down to the beard, sandals, and brown homespun habit, were it not for the officious guards inside the basilica. Taking pictures, they seemed to feel, was frivolous and disrespectful. Yet they tried with some difficulty to preserve a solemn, hushed, atmosphere inside the church by bellowing "No foto! No foto!" over a PA system, repeatedly booming the admonition over the praying faithful all day.

Orvieto, it turned out, was a tranquil revelation. Orvieto hits that sweet spot between small town and big city. It's large enough to feature interesting shops, terrific restaurants, and cultural icons like the Duomo, but small enough to be human scale, blessedly free of traffic in its old quarter, and a delight to walk in. It also is comparatively quiet—a real plus to any who have spent a summer afternoon in Rome wandering around the Spanish Steps or the Colosseum among sweating tourists and honking cars.

The Orvieto cathedral dominates the hillside on which it is built and greets first-time viewers with a breathtaking bang when they emerge from Orvieto's narrow streets into the main church square. Soaring skyward, the Duomo makes a stunning first impression with its seemingly contradictory exterior. This contradiction is understandable, since construction of the church began in the late thirteenth century, on the orders of Pope Urban IV, and was not completed until three centuries later, in 1591, spanning several periods of architecture and design. In fact, installation of the final bit of major construction—a set of three huge bronze doors to replace older wooden ones—didn't happen until 1970.

The ornate front of the church is arguably one of the most stunning examples of Gothic architecture in the world, and is widely viewed as one of the great masterpieces of the late Middle Ages. Attributed to Sienese sculptor and architect Lorenzo Maitani, the towering facade blends gilt and intricate decoration with four pillars, two pointed Gothic arches, one central rounded Romanesque arch, a large rose window, as well as realistically—not to say disturbingly—carved bas reliefs depicting biblical tales from the Book of Genesis to the Last Judgment in the Book of Revelation. These sculptures were placed near eye level at the base of the facade and served as cautionary tales to a largely illiterate, yet faithful, public. Even today, the writhing, naked figures of those condemned to eternity in hell at the Last Judgment are difficult to view.

By contrast, the older sides of the building, featuring alternating straight rows of white travertine and dark-grey basalt, are stolidly Romanesque and appear to be almost austere and, ironically, modern. Somehow, it all hangs together as these mostly horizontal lines direct one's attention on the church's magnificent front. The side walls of the Duomo undulate with rounded windows and other elements, never straying from the strict linear design of the basalt and travertine stripes. Even one of the Duomo's earliest architectural errors is dressed in these stripes. During initial construction, the architect Maitani decided to strengthen the external walls of the cathedral with flying buttresses—a new feature of the emerging Gothic period—but these ultimately proved to be ineffectual. Rather than tear them down, later builders simply incorporated them into the walls of newly built transept chapels.

Today, the flying buttresses are clearly visible from the outside, lending a fly-caught-in-amber aspect to the already arresting design.

Another thing that always intrigued me was that the stark motif of the light and dark stripes carried over to the interior of the cathedral itself. I don't know when I ever have seen this done so dramatically—but it works beautifully inside the church as well as outside.

One reason for this is that there is virtually nothing inside the cathedral's main entranceway to compete with the design, which is reflected not just in the church's interior walls but in a succession of mammoth support pillars that go the length of the cathedral nave. Travel writer Rick Steves notes, "the nave feels spacious and less cluttered than those in most Italian churches. It used to be filled with statues and fancy chapels until 1877, when the people decided they wanted to 'un-Baroque' their church." I should note that in recent years, more and more statues have returned to the interior, but judiciously placed between the gargantuan pillars, they still leave the cathedral's vast main interior largely empty.

The sense of peace one gets inside the cathedral is palpable. Without a succession of paintings or sculpture to compete for your attention, one is left simply to contemplate the vast quiet openness of this consecrated space. In all the times I have been there, it never fails to astonish. It also helps that the interior is bathed in warm light filtered through alabaster panes in the bottom parts of the cathedral's side windows (the upper parts are more traditional stained glass).

This is not to say that the Duomo of Orvieto is simply a big striped box. In fact, the chapel of San Brizio, on the right side of the main altar, boasts some of the most amazing frescoes in all of Italy, painted by Luca Signorelli (c. 1450–1523), the Italian Renaissance master who was an inspiration to a young Michelangelo.

One easily could call the Signorelli frescoes the highlight of the Orvieto cathedral, surpassing even the Chapel of the Corporal across the way, where the reliquary houses a thirteenth-century communion cloth said to have been stained by a bleeding consecrated communion host. (The appearance of the blood was seen as affirmation of Catholic doctrine that communion bread and wine become the body and blood of Christ at the moment of consecration.)

Signorelli's frescoes depict dramatically the Day of Judgment and Life After Death, including even an antichrist being whispered to by a serpentine devil. Again, these ancient artworks were designed to instill devotion, as well as fear, in the faithful, but they also reflect a master painter's ability to render human form and to tell stories through human actions and gestures, and not through obscure religious symbolism.

There is drama in every one of the frescoes, and you are swept along in this compelling depiction of the end times. You feel exultation at the assumption of the righteous into heaven and dread at how well Signorelli depicts the descent of the damned into hell.

And, if all of that is too overwhelming, as you leave the Duomo and emerge into the sunlight, my favorite gelato place is just a block or so away on the right (check out the nocciola).

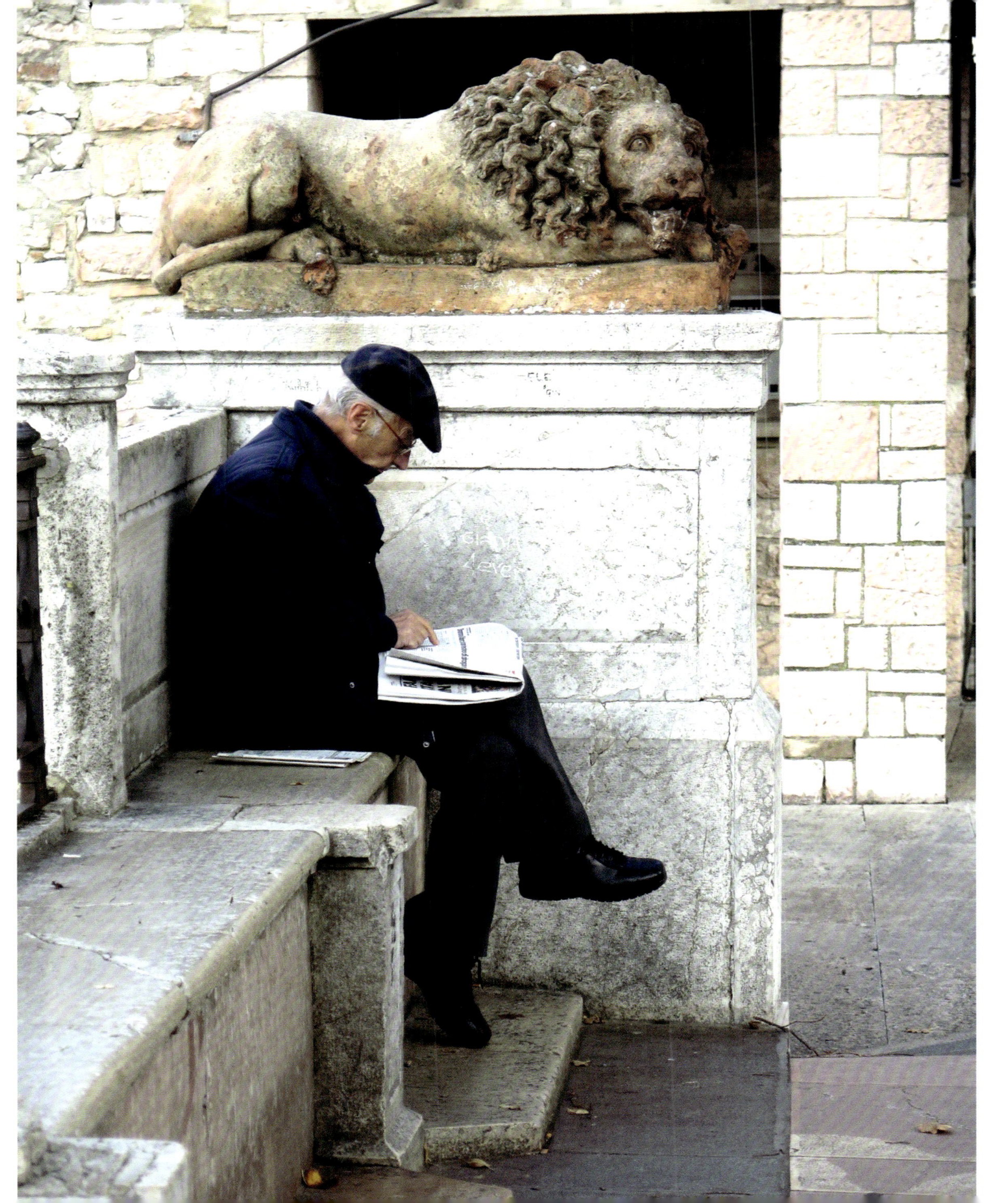

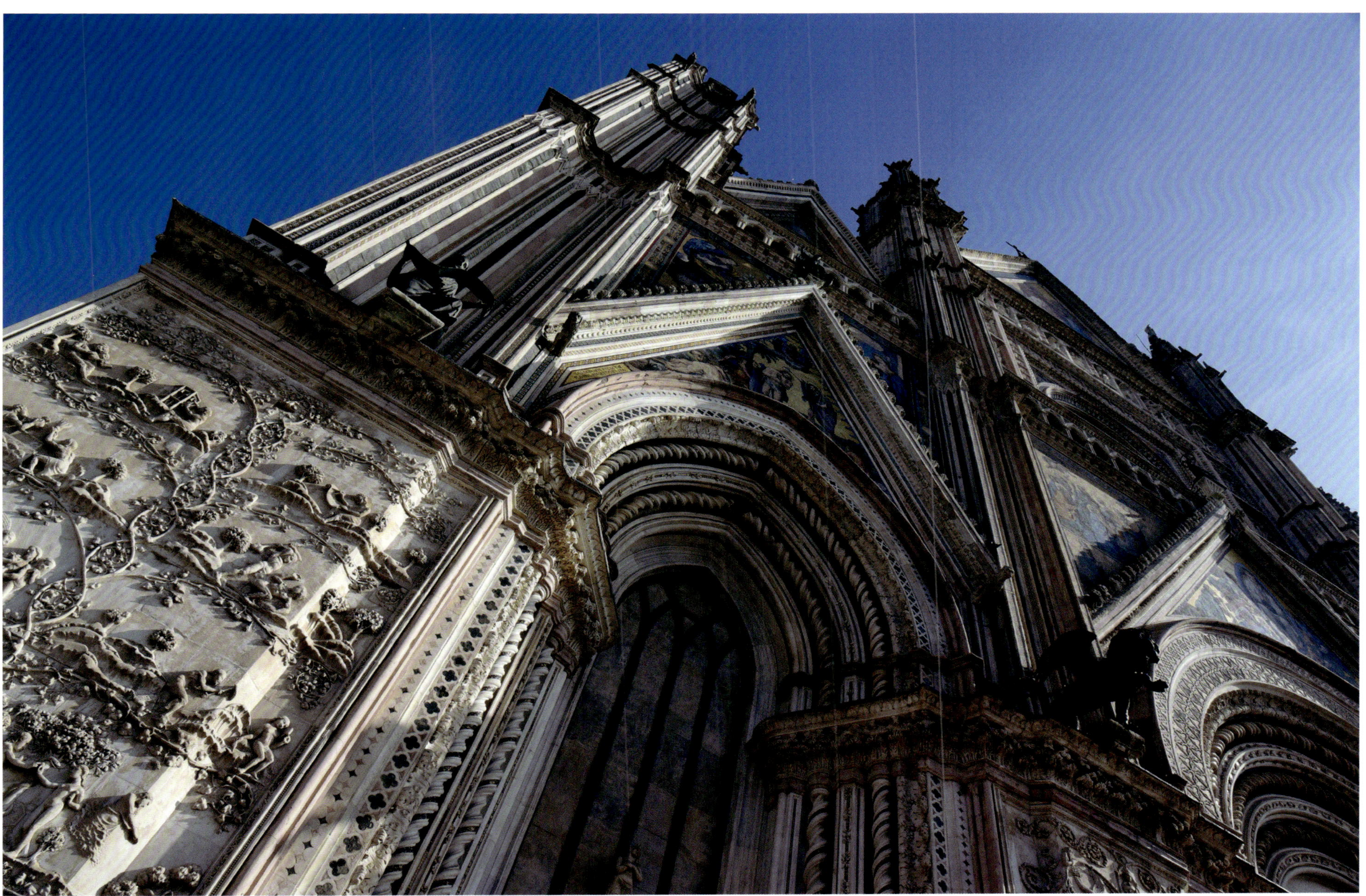

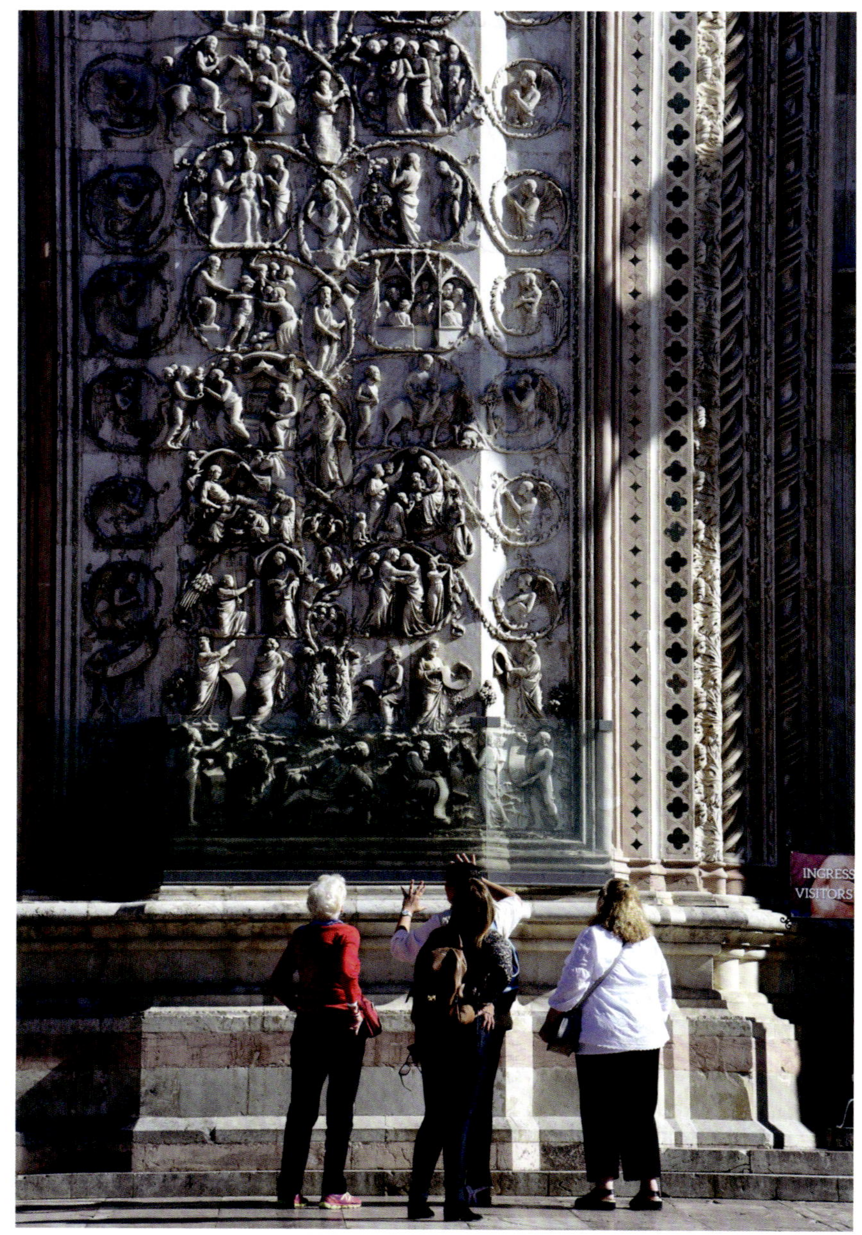
INGRESS
VISITORS

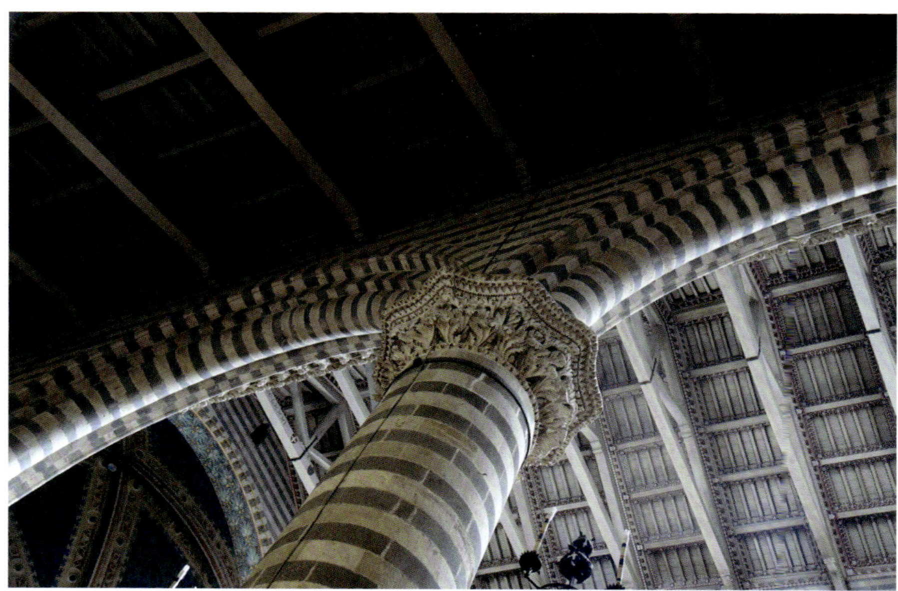

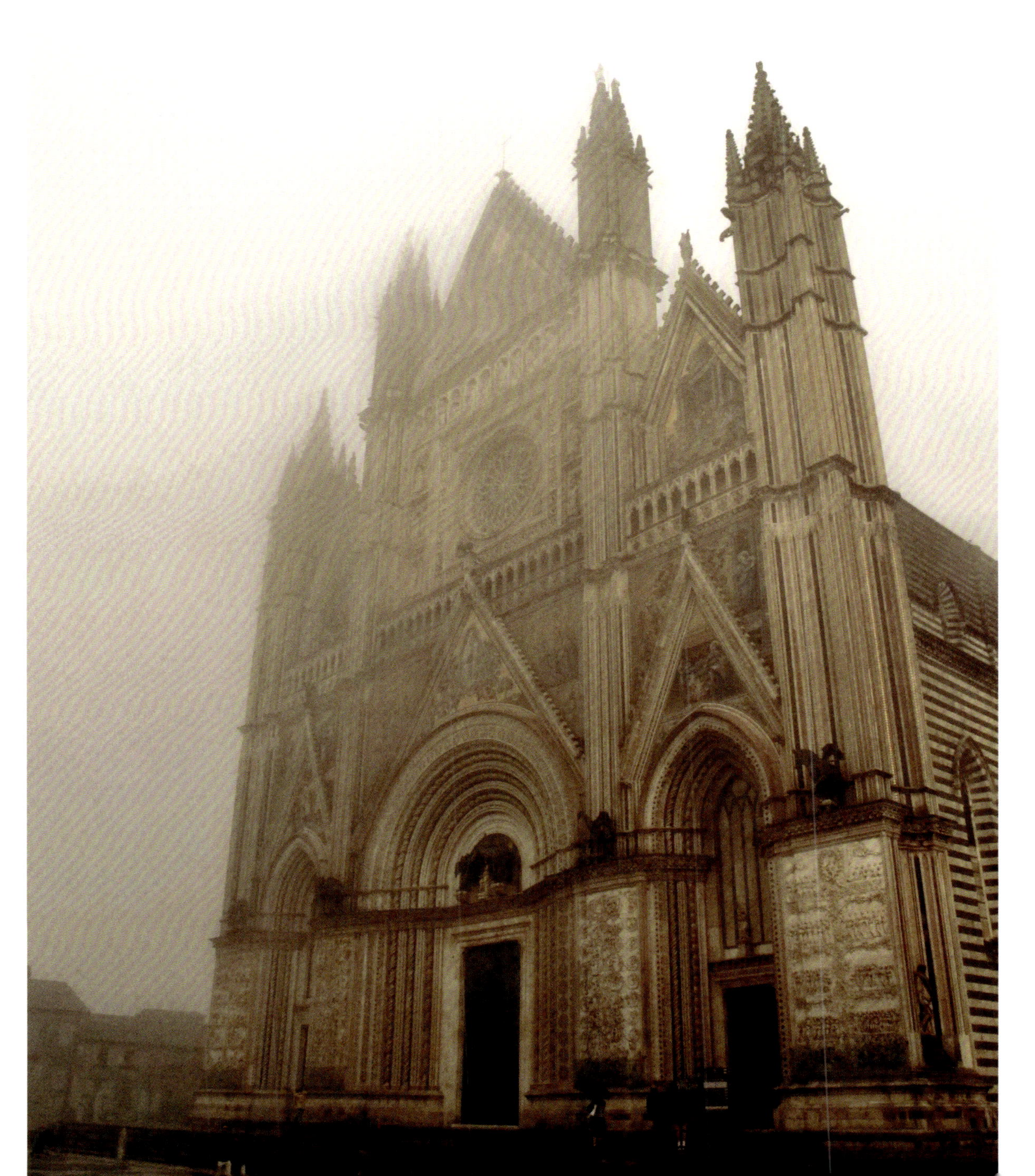

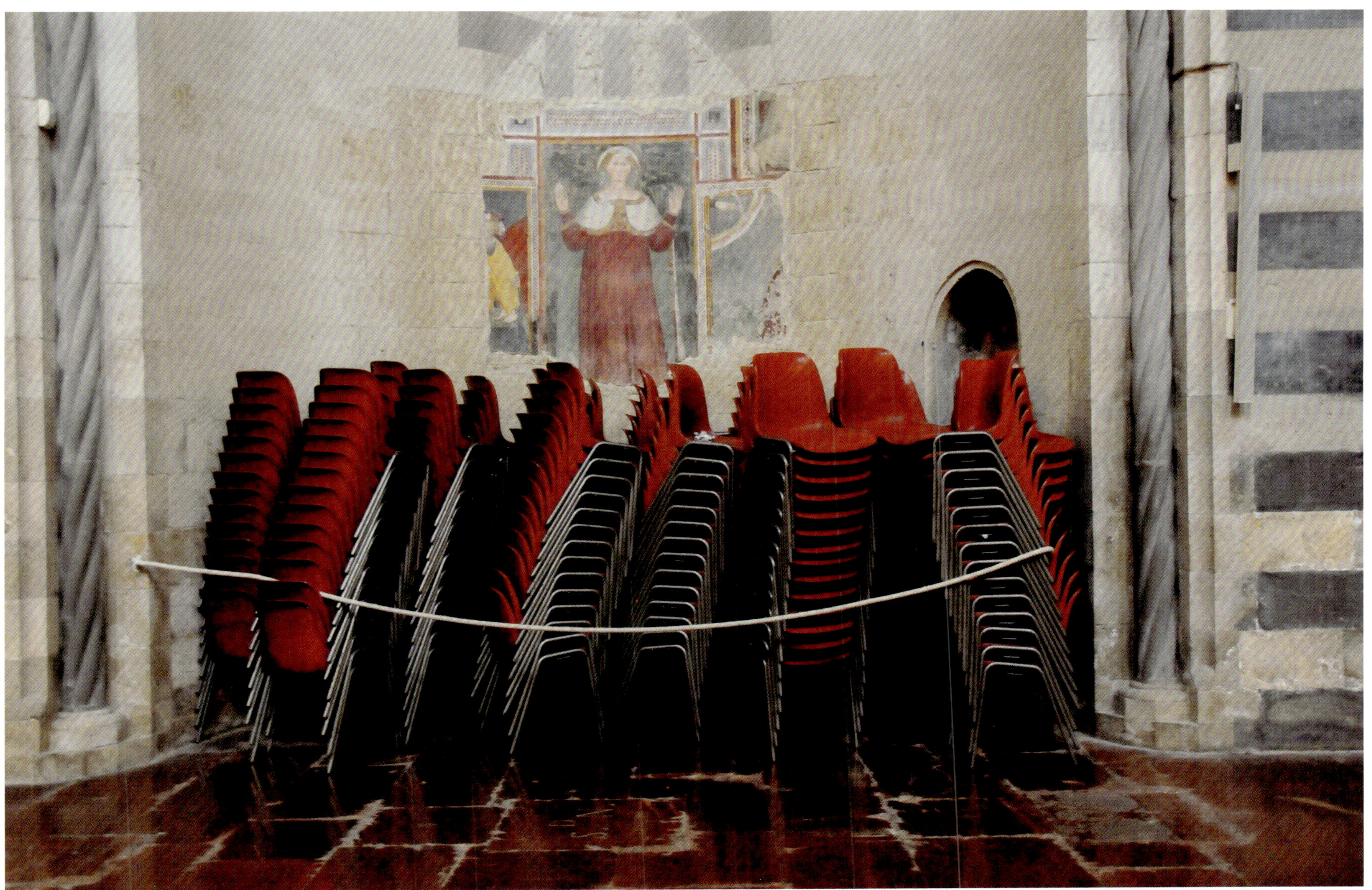

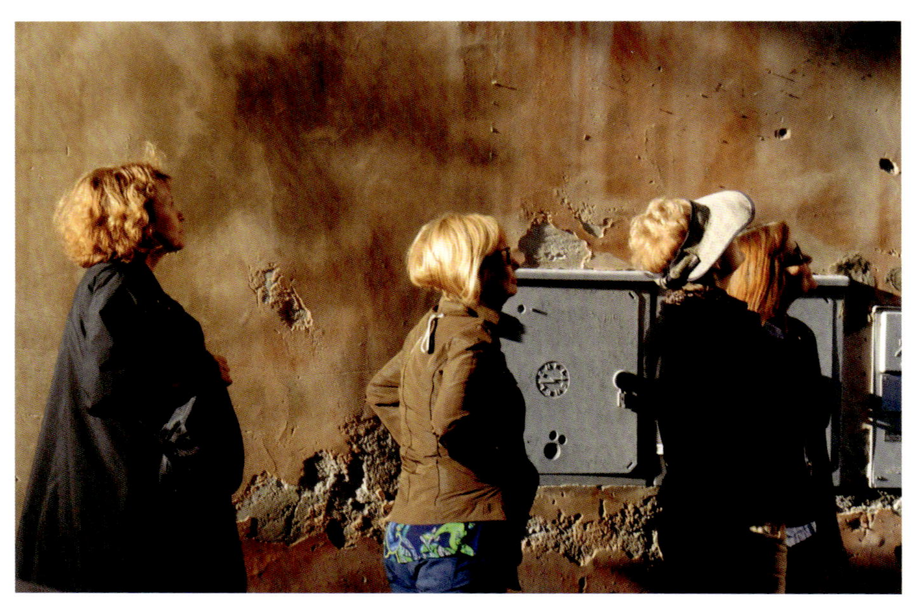

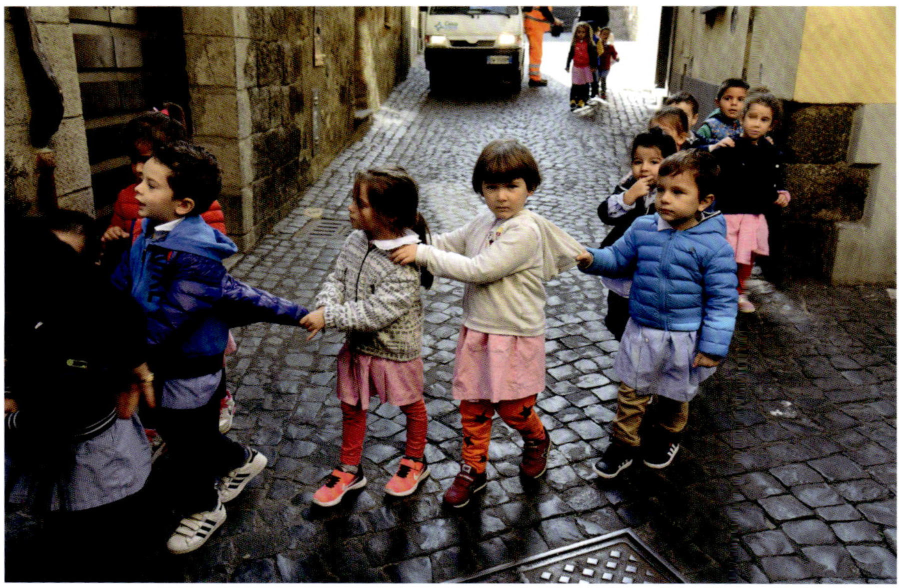

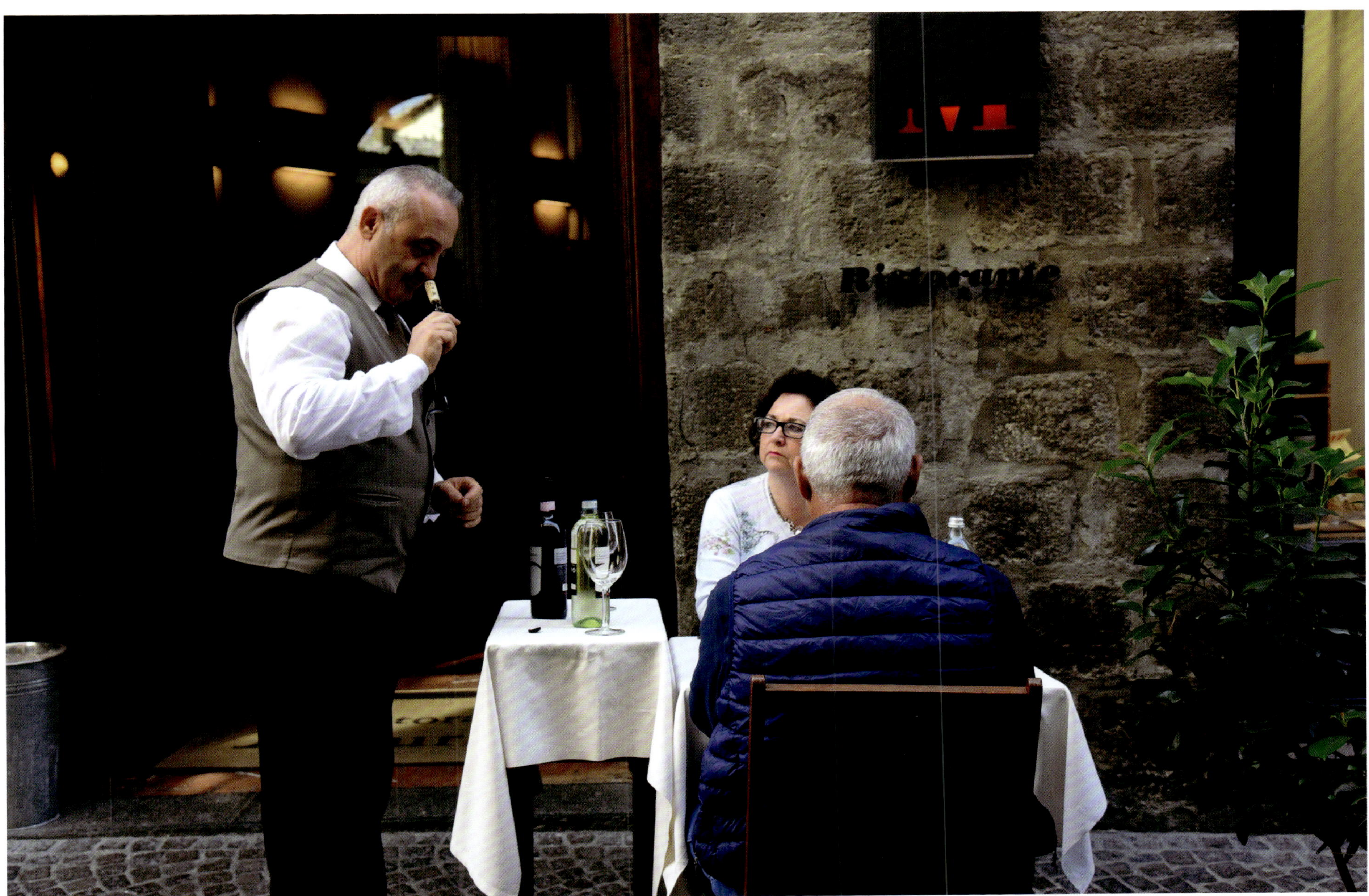

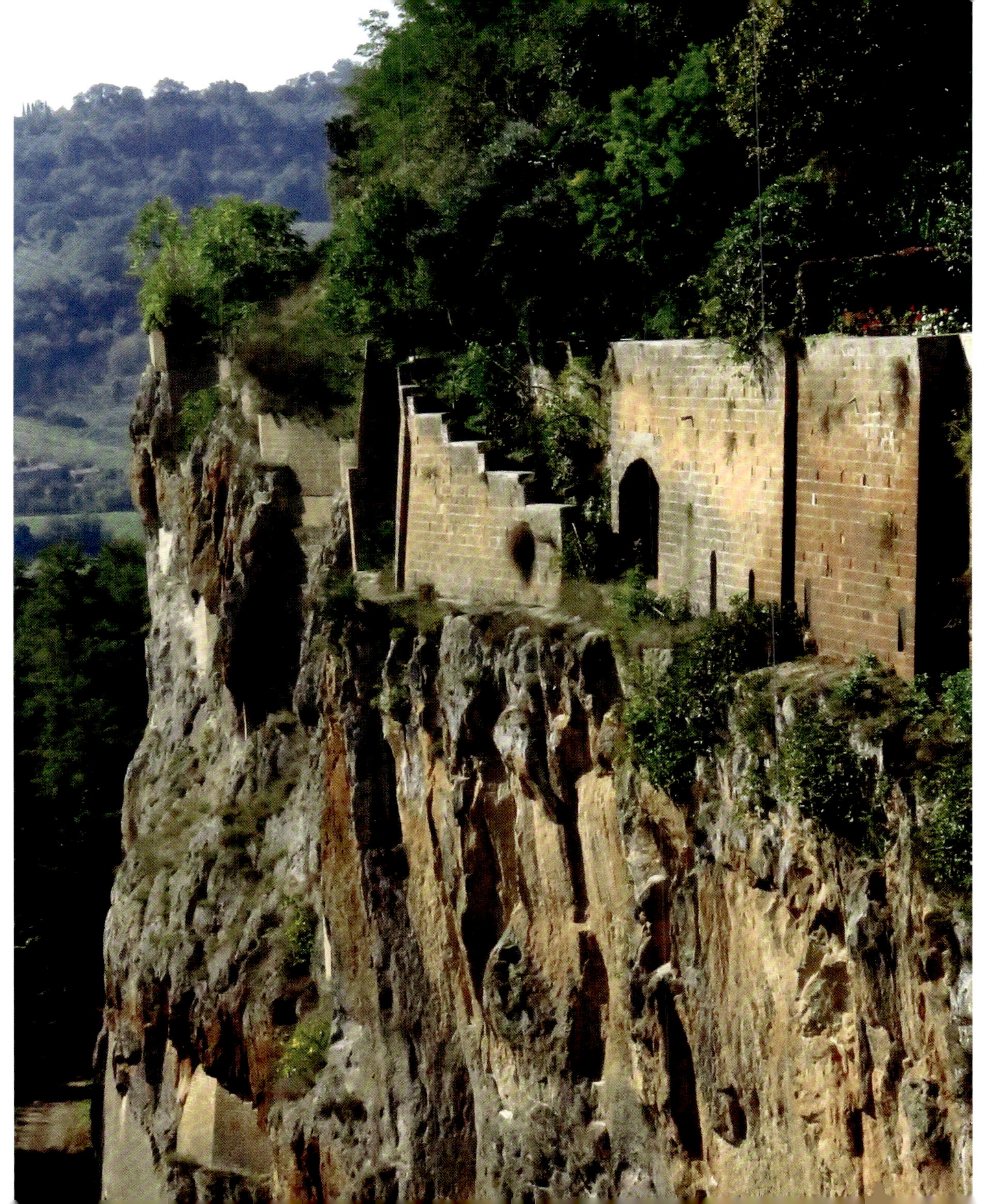

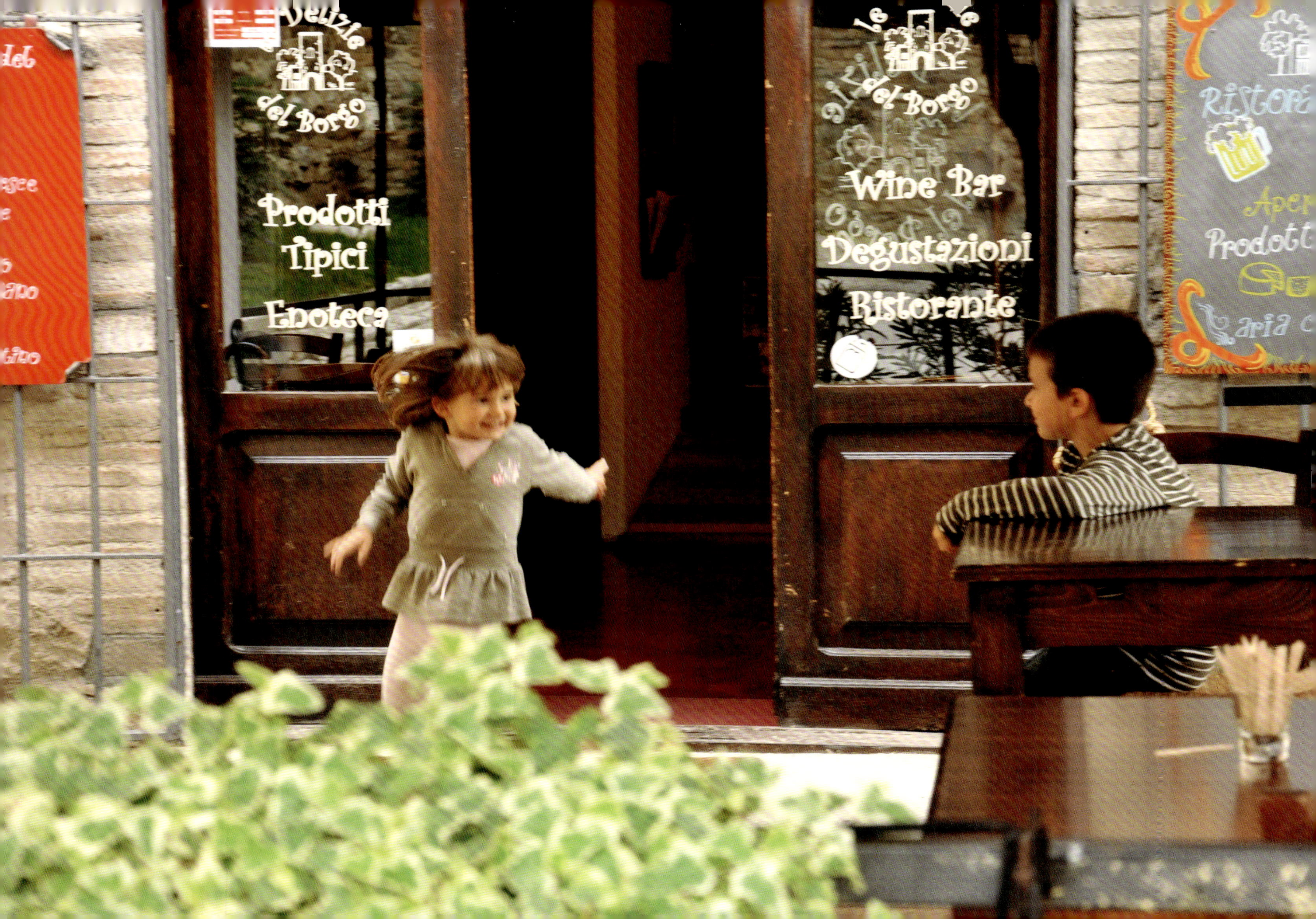

Delizie del Borgo
Prodotti Tipici
Enoteca
Wine Bar
Degustazioni
Ristorante

Bevagna, and Italy's Brigadoon

They are two very small towns in Italy, and each took hold of us as soon as we saw them, but in different ways. We came to Bevagna through a friend who knew the owner of a restaurant, Le Delizie del Borgo (the delicacies of the village). That first meeting blossomed into annual feasts at Simone Proietti Pesci's homey trattoria, first located just inside the town wall and later just outside, in an airy new space in a quiet public park.

By contrast, Judy and I first heard of Civita di Bagnoregio decades earlier, on our honeymoon in Venice in 1984. "Oh, you must go to Civita," we were told. And we did—to our amazement.

Just outside of Umbria in Lazio, Civita di Bagnoregio is a frozen-in-amber Italian hill town that is Italy's Brigadoon. An unforgiving nature carved away much of the porous tufa on which the town was built so that all that remains is a small collection of ancient buildings: one church, a handful of homes and gardens, and a smattering of shops and restaurants, all perched on a hilltop and accessible only by a very long pedestrian footbridge. On a foggy morning you can see just the town floating in the sky. It is magical— like Brigadoon.

It was in Bevagna that life seemed to unfold languidly before us, and in sometimes interesting ways: an outdoor flea market, where Judy bought a homemade (and humane) animal trap that she turned into a sculpture; a nonna in fire-engine-red curls navigating the town's narrow streets with aplomb—on a Segway.

Italy's Brigadoon

It sits atop a small mountain of volcanic stone, accessible only by footbridge, its miniature towers set against an azure sky.

You look at it from afar and, at first, you cannot believe what you are seeing. But in fact, Civita di Bagnoregio, arguably the smallest and most unspoiled of Italian hill towns, does exist—even if it is called "la citta che muore," the city that is dying.

For one thing, you can't get anywhere near it by car—you must traverse a long uphill pedestrian bridge to even get to the town walls. The town itself seems to float against the sky in the distance, so the parallel is unmistakable: this is Italy's Brigadoon.

Yet for a place that was founded by the Etruscans some 2,500 years ago, and later ruled by the Romans, Civita today seems remarkably vibrant, if also ecologically threatened.

If the city is dying, it certainly will be a magnificent corpse. This is not your average Italian hill town, like, say, Todi, where there is bustling life within its ancient walls. Or Orvieto, where a magnificent cathedral anchors the town's center. Or even Montefalco, where the breathtaking views have earned it the sobriquet "the balcony of Umbria."

Truth to tell, once you walk the long uphill footbridge, you come to Civita's charming, though tiny, town square, and little else.

But that's the point. The term "unspoiled" can be overused, but it applies here. Cast your eye away from the several first-class restaurants and cafes that cater to the tourists, and you have walked back centuries in time. No open-air markets, no drugstores, no post office, no ATMs—and certainly no cars. (The only motorized vehicles that can navigate the footbridge, bringing supplies and food to restaurants and shops, for example, are tiny three-wheeled runabouts.)

"Civita is an artist's dream, a town in the nude," says travel writer Rick Steves. Without doubt, he adds, it is his favorite Italian hill town.

The Renaissance largely bypassed Civita, so what you see there is largely medieval, and because of that, breathtaking, if not also unique. Located two hours from Rome in the north of Lazio in Italy's center, and near the Umbrian border, Civita is as isolated as it is (again, think of the mythical Brigadoon) because of erosion and earthquake. Where once a pathway for donkeys linked Civita with its larger, more stable neighbor, Bagnoregio, below, now there is only the comparatively narrow footbridge granting access to the sparsely populated town. How sparse? In winter, the permanent population fluctuates between six and twelve; at the height of tourist season, its inhabitants may reach only one hundred.

Among these was Allessandro Michele, the forty-four-year-old fashion tyro who was named in 2015 to be Gucci's new creative director. Michele, and his partner Giovanni Attili, a professor of urban planning, understandably fell in love with Civita, then lovingly restored and decorated what became their country house, built from the ruins of an old monastery, sitting over a network of Etruscan caves.

Visiting Civita for the first time, one is aware not only of the beauty but of the quiet. With none of the noise of modern life from cars, buses, boom boxes, large tour groups, etc., you relax—and, if you are smart, revel in the surprising tranquility.

This is a place where you linger over your espresso or aperitivo at an open-air bar or bruschetteria and realize that the only ambient noise is from footsteps and conversation. A cadre of resident cats and kittens usually can be counted on for comic relief. And a walk behind any of the town's thick stone walls usually will offer up a stunning and well-tended garden.

When Judy and I first ventured to Civita on our honeymoon in 1984 the place seemed, if anything, more medieval than it does today. We probably were the only tourists there that day—there was almost no one in the streets and the place was all but deserted. Wandering down a hill at one point, we spied a garden and a small cave, its entrance enclosed by a fence. Inside was a huge pig that did not seem friendly. We did not linger.

Civita's public square is dominated by the modest Catholic Church of San Donato. It was built centuries ago over the ruins of an Etruscan, and later, Roman, temple. In fact, Rick Steves notes that you can see remnants of the pillars of these pagan temples "sitting like barstools" in front of San Donato's simple, elegant entrance.

Inside, the church is a surprisingly open, inviting, and, in the hot summer, a pleasantly cool place to pass an hour or so, poring over its several treasures. One year I encountered an elderly man sitting cross-legged on the church's floor, sketchpad in hand, intently drawing the church's ornate baptismal font. He was a retired priest who had fallen in love with Civita years earlier and now returned regularly to draw and to paint.

The church also features relics of its two patron saints. An urn containing the ashes of the martyred Santa Vittoria is displayed at the left altar. On the right, and far more dramatic, are the reliquary remains of Sant' Ildebrando (Saint Hildebrand), the town's ninth-century bishop. He is laid out in full regalia in a glass coffin so that visitors can gaze on his waxy face and beard. Among the legends surrounding Hildebrand is the one of his resurrecting a cooked partridge, given to him for dinner as he lay old and sick. Noting that it happened to be a time of fasting, Hildebrand is said to have prayed over the bird until it was revived and took flight.

Civita's most famous son was San Bonaventura (Saint Bonaventure), who was born in the town around 1221 and is credited with helping to sustain the order of St. Francis in the years after that most famous of Italian saints founded it. Born Giovanni Fidanza, he was said to have been healed as a child by Francis, who blessed him with a new name, "O Buona Ventura," in effect predicting a bright future for the boy.

For centuries, great chunks of Civita have been falling away into the Tiber valley. Today, you literally can see ancient walls with windows facing the sky, seemingly at the town's edge. But that's only because the rest of the building behind the windows has collapsed.

The volcanic tufa on which the town is built is porous and friable, meaning geologically unstable. In addition, erosion and the passage of centuries have contributed to the honeycomb of caves on which the city rests. This can be a mixed blessing. During World War II, these caves served as bomb shelters, and many serve now as perfect wine cellars. But caves, of course, can collapse. There are plans to reinforce the plateau on which Civita rests with steel rods, and today you can see sophisticated measuring devices that monitor any movement.

There also is a serious move afoot to place the city on UNESCO's list of World Heritage Sites. The campaign already has garnered support from many of Italy's political and artistic elite, who argue that so unique a place in Italy, if not the world, must be preserved for future generations. Being a World Heritage Site would make Civita eligible for more restoration and preservation money, but the entire vetting process takes time—something Civita does not have.

Still, in an age when plastic and disposable are the norm, there are plenty who would argue that surely this is a place worth saving, no matter how long it takes.

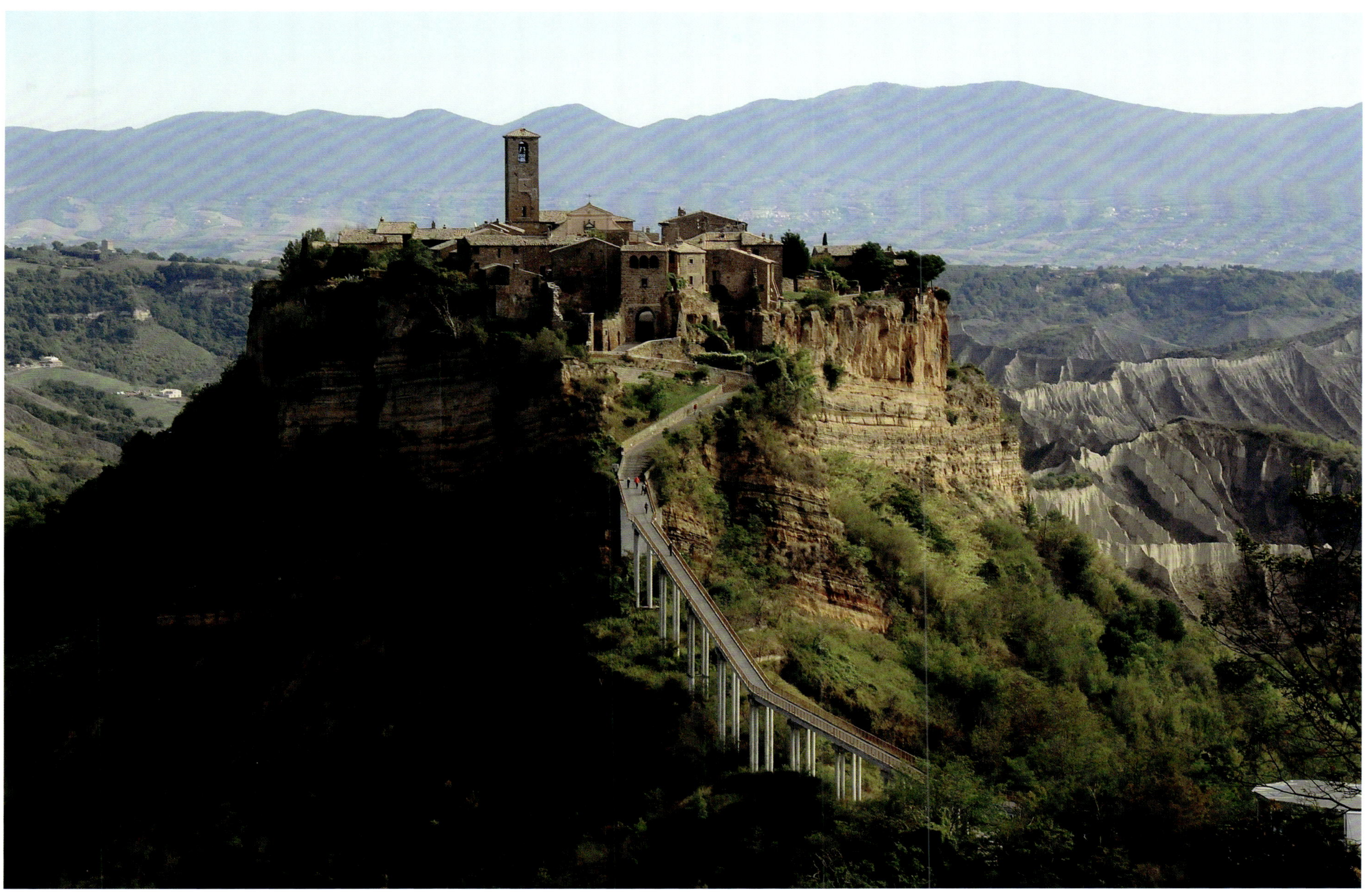

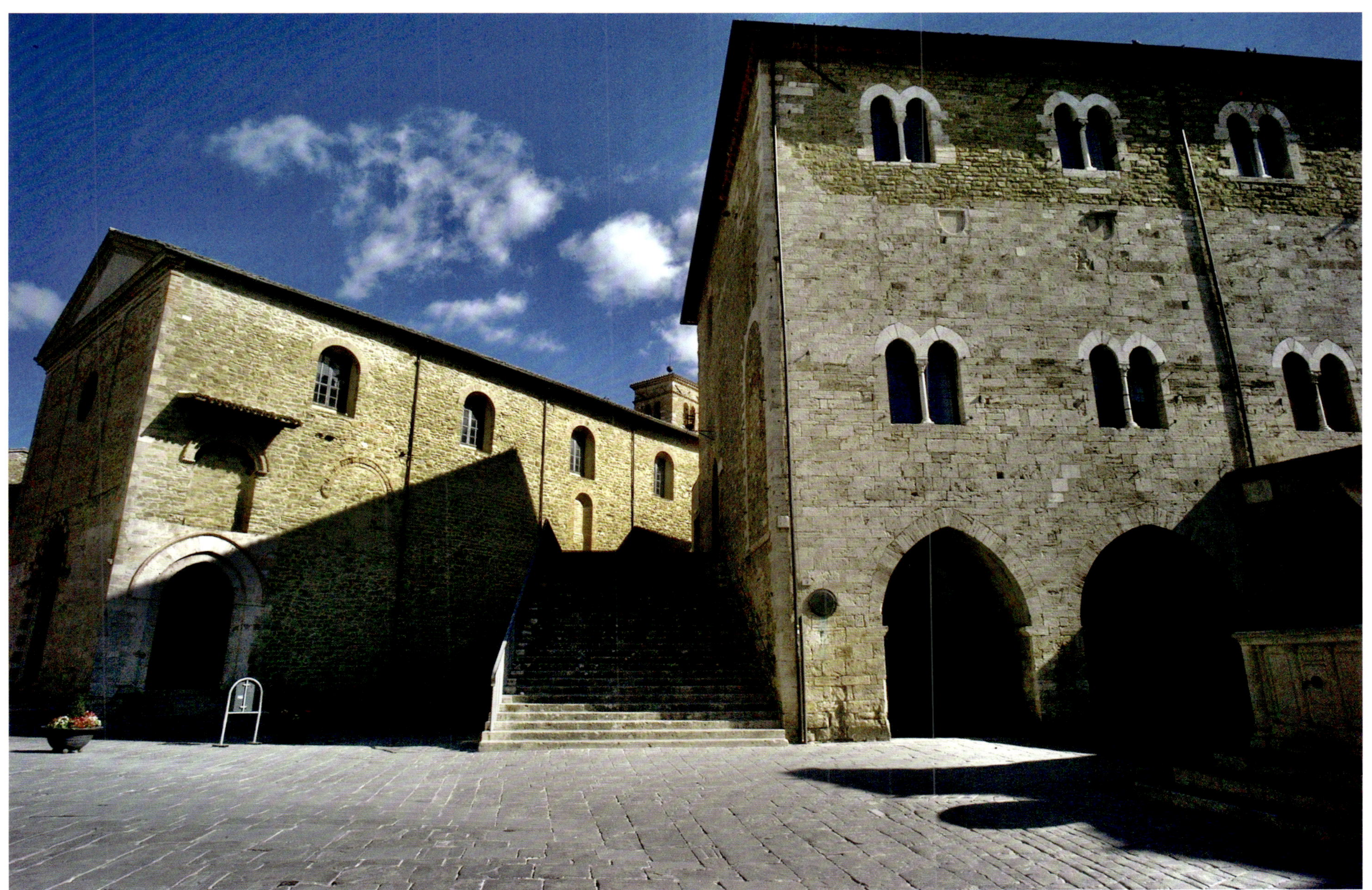

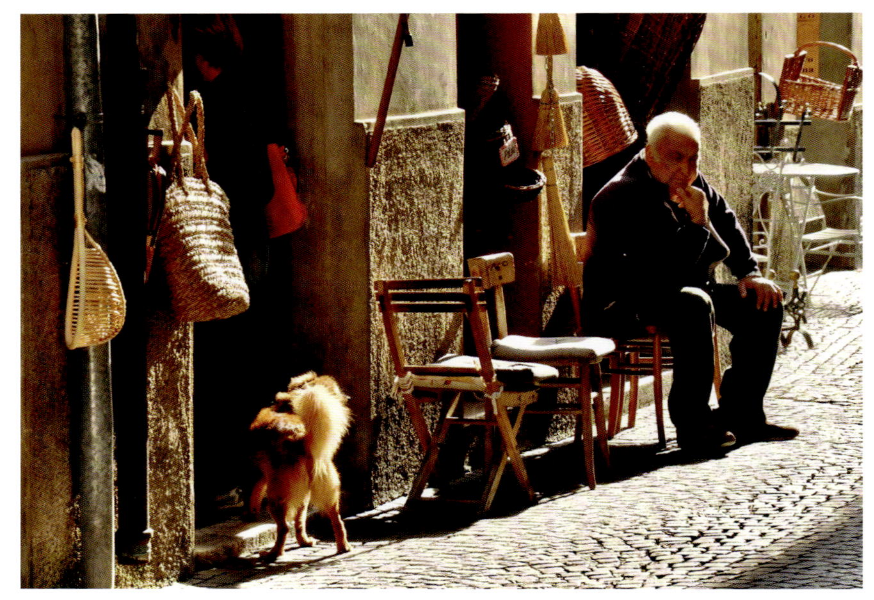

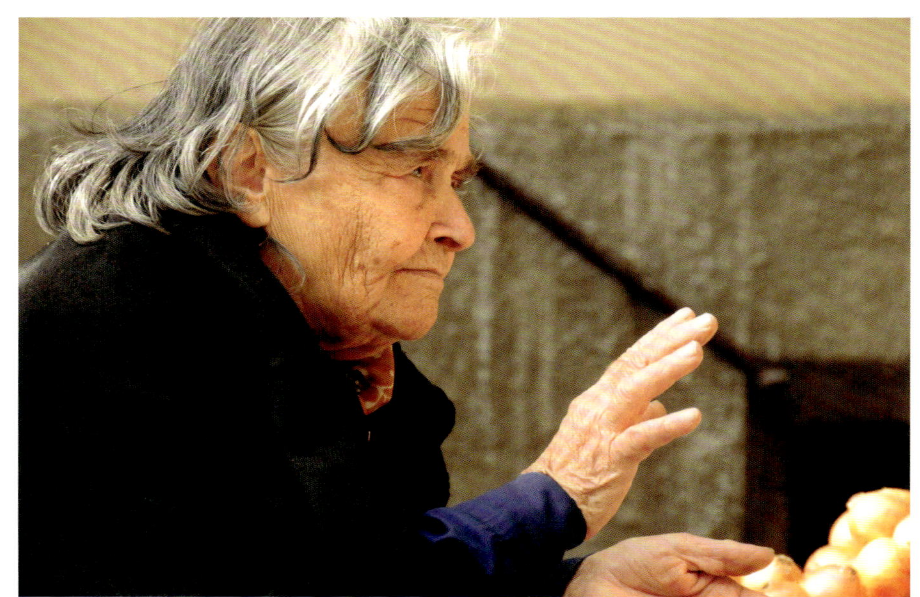

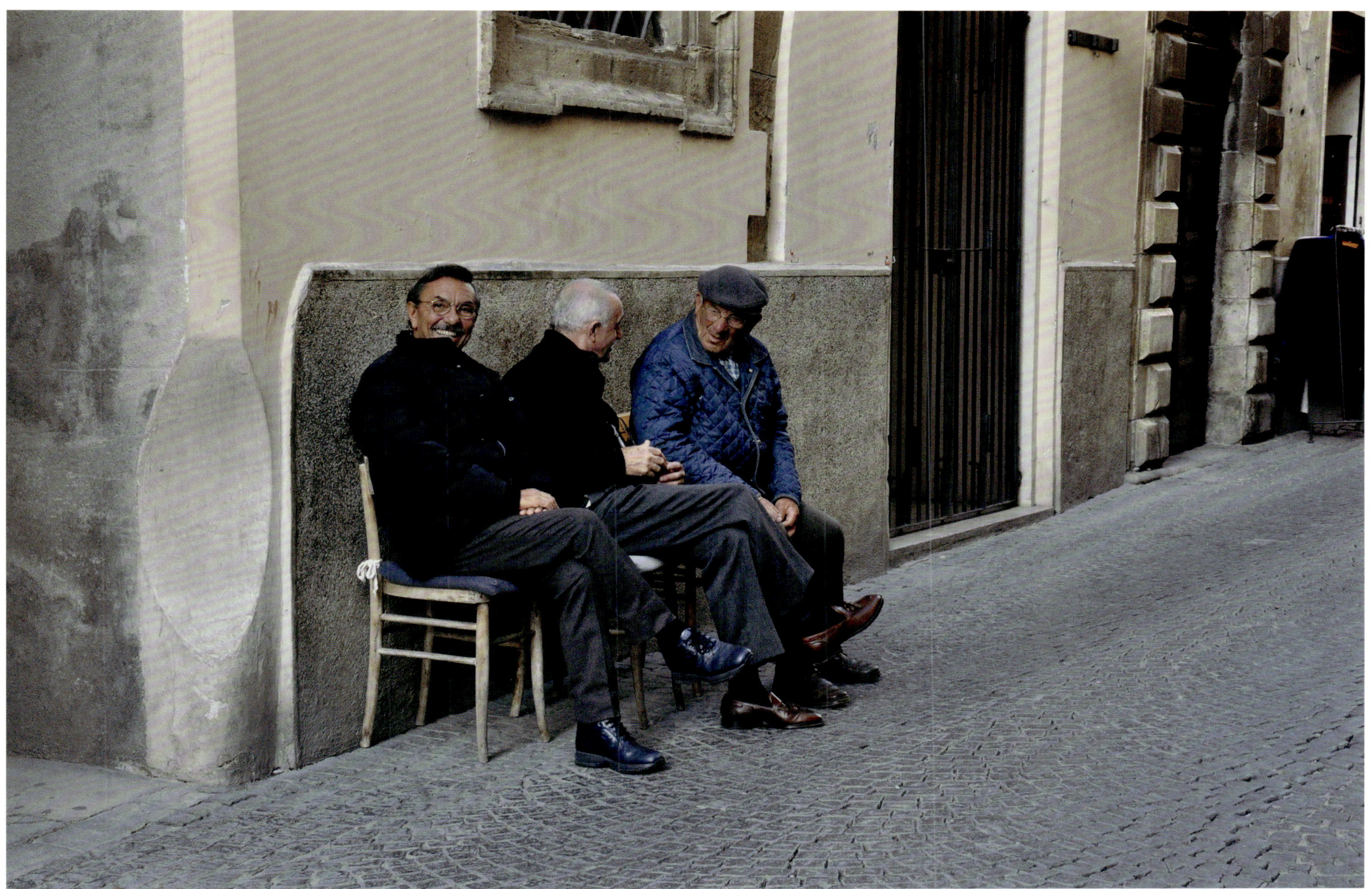

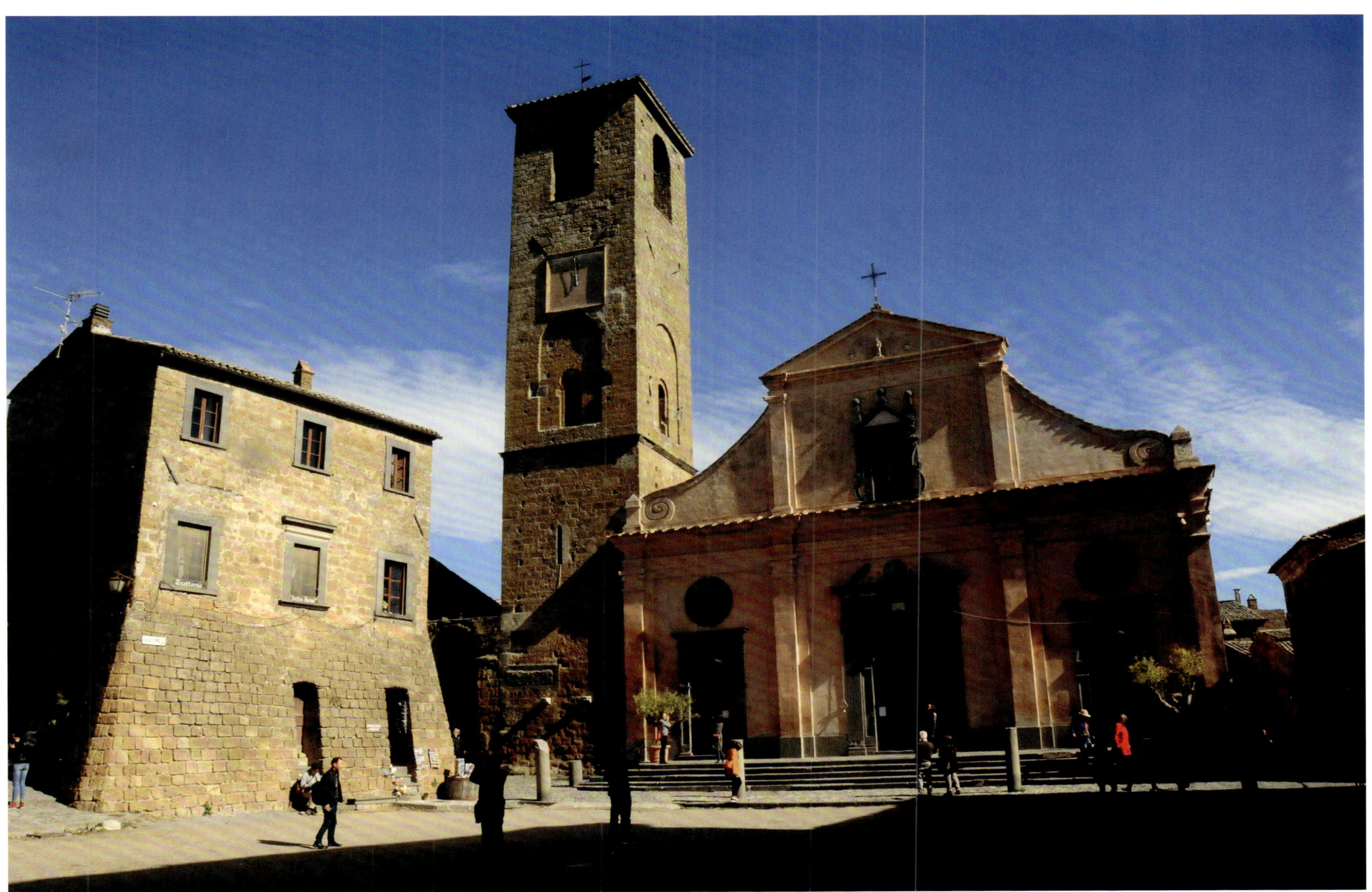

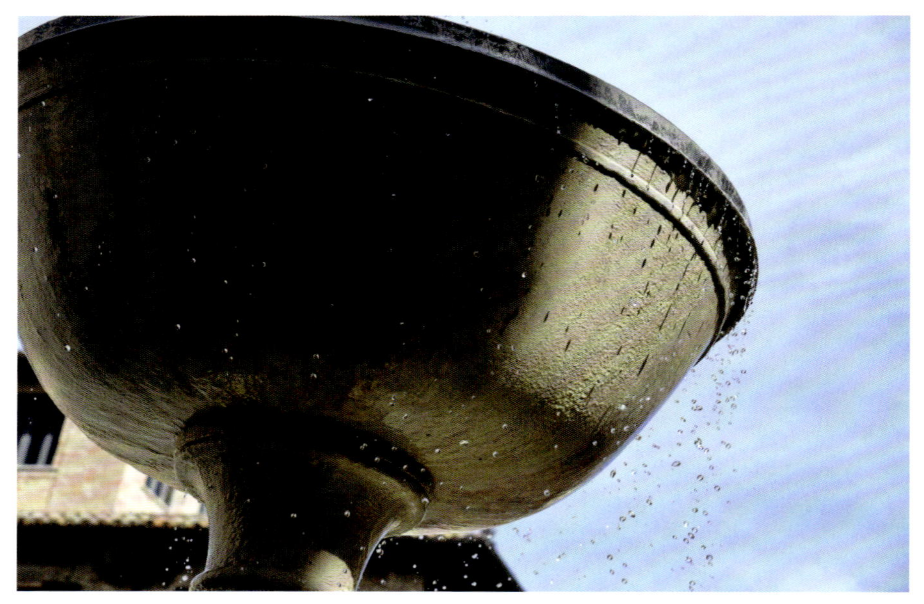

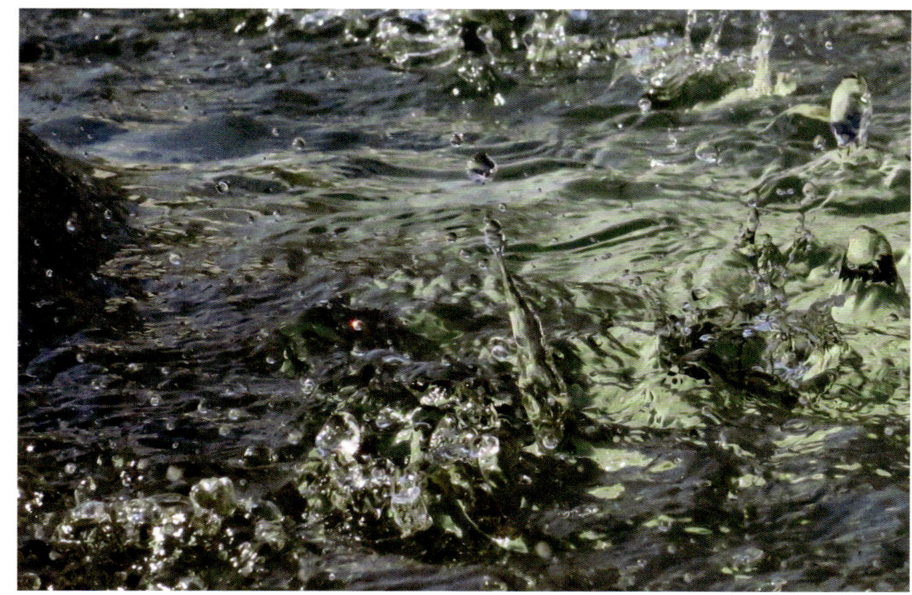

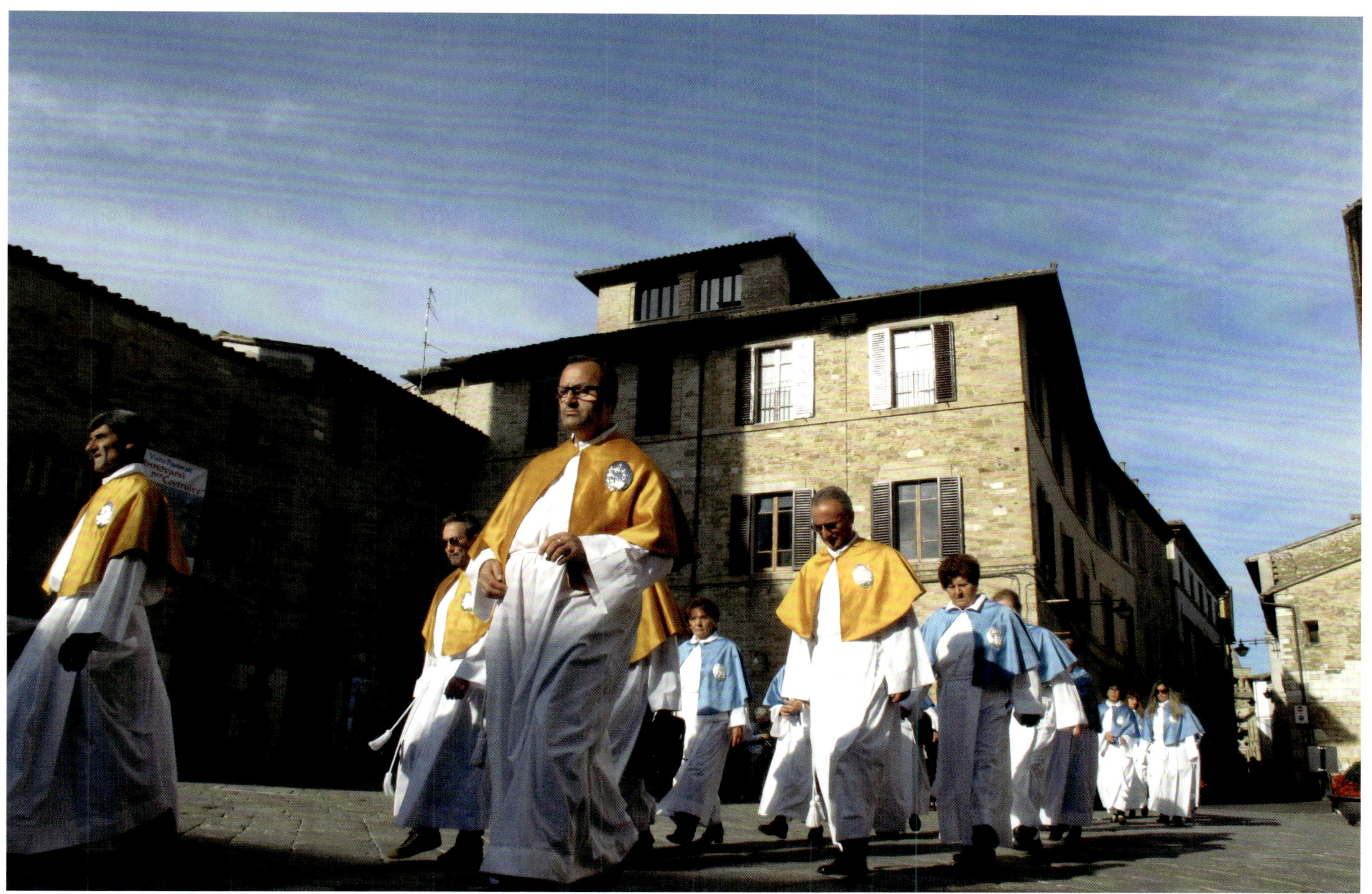

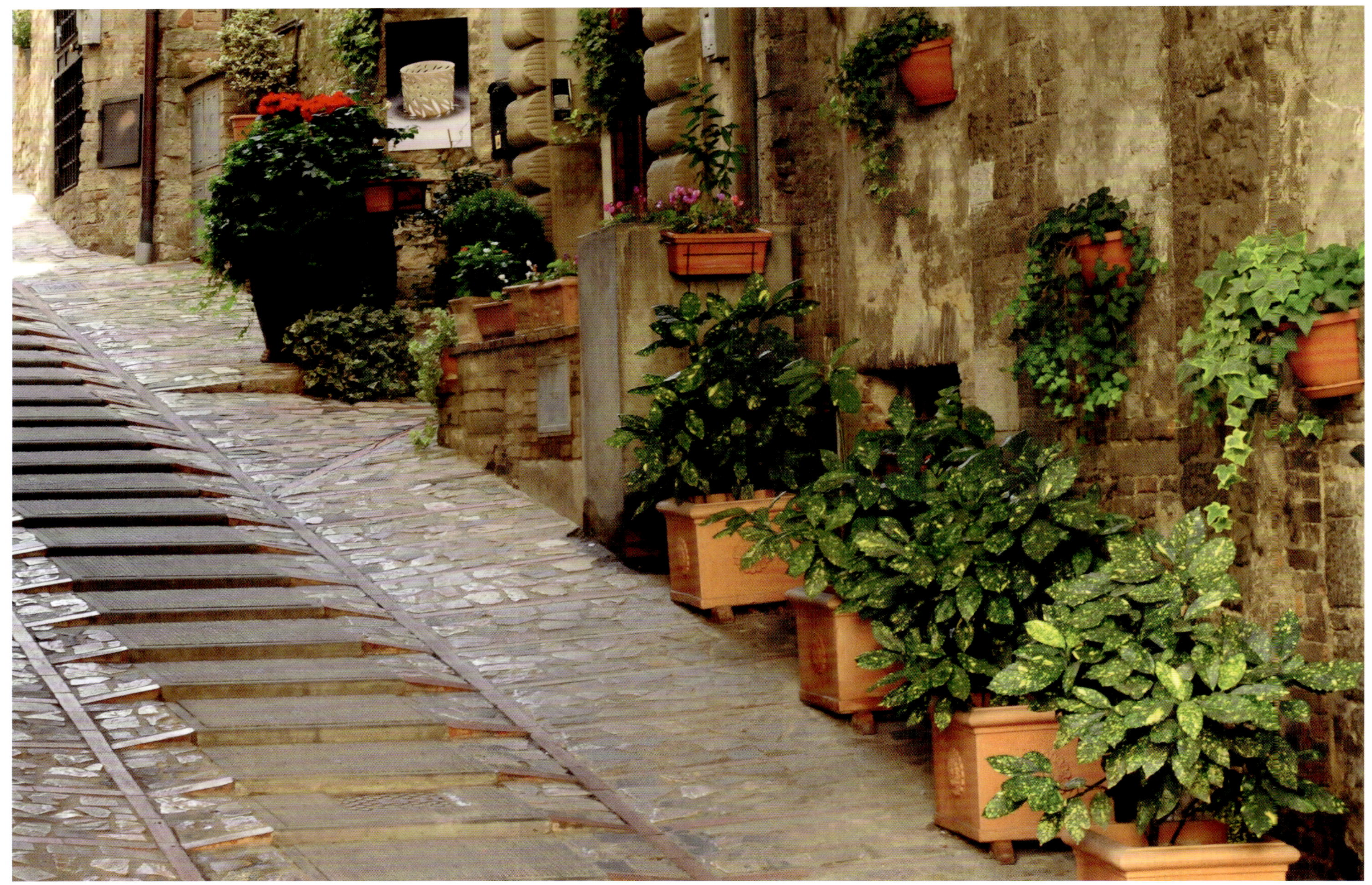

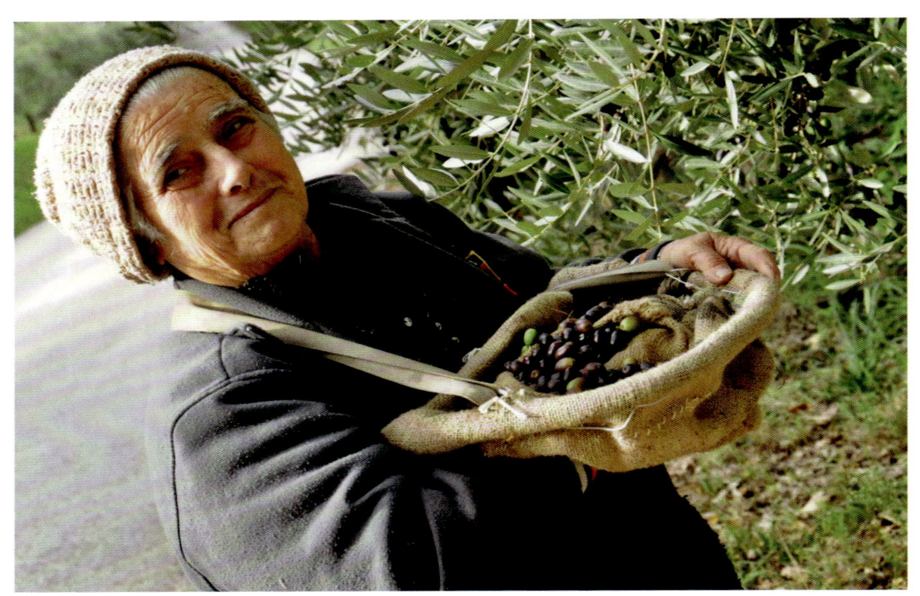

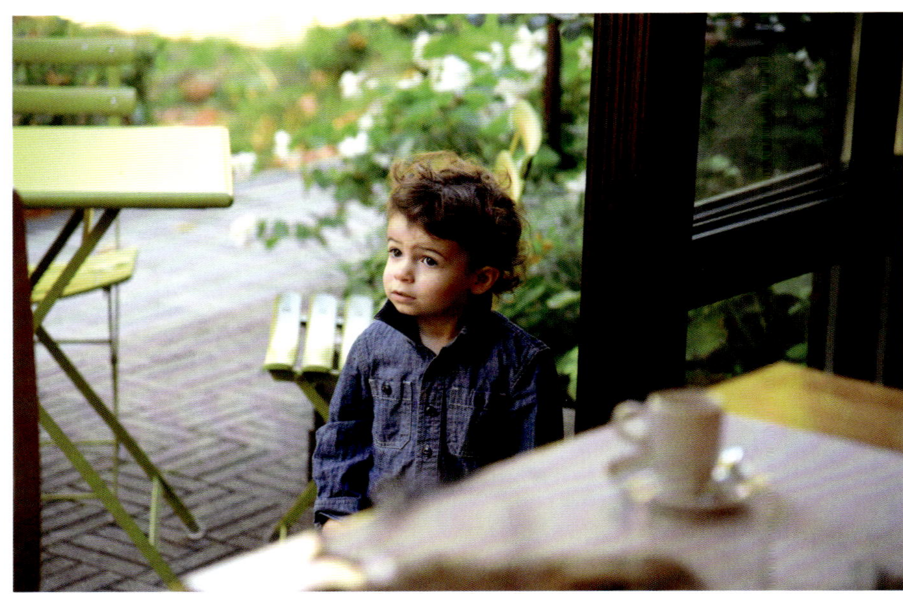

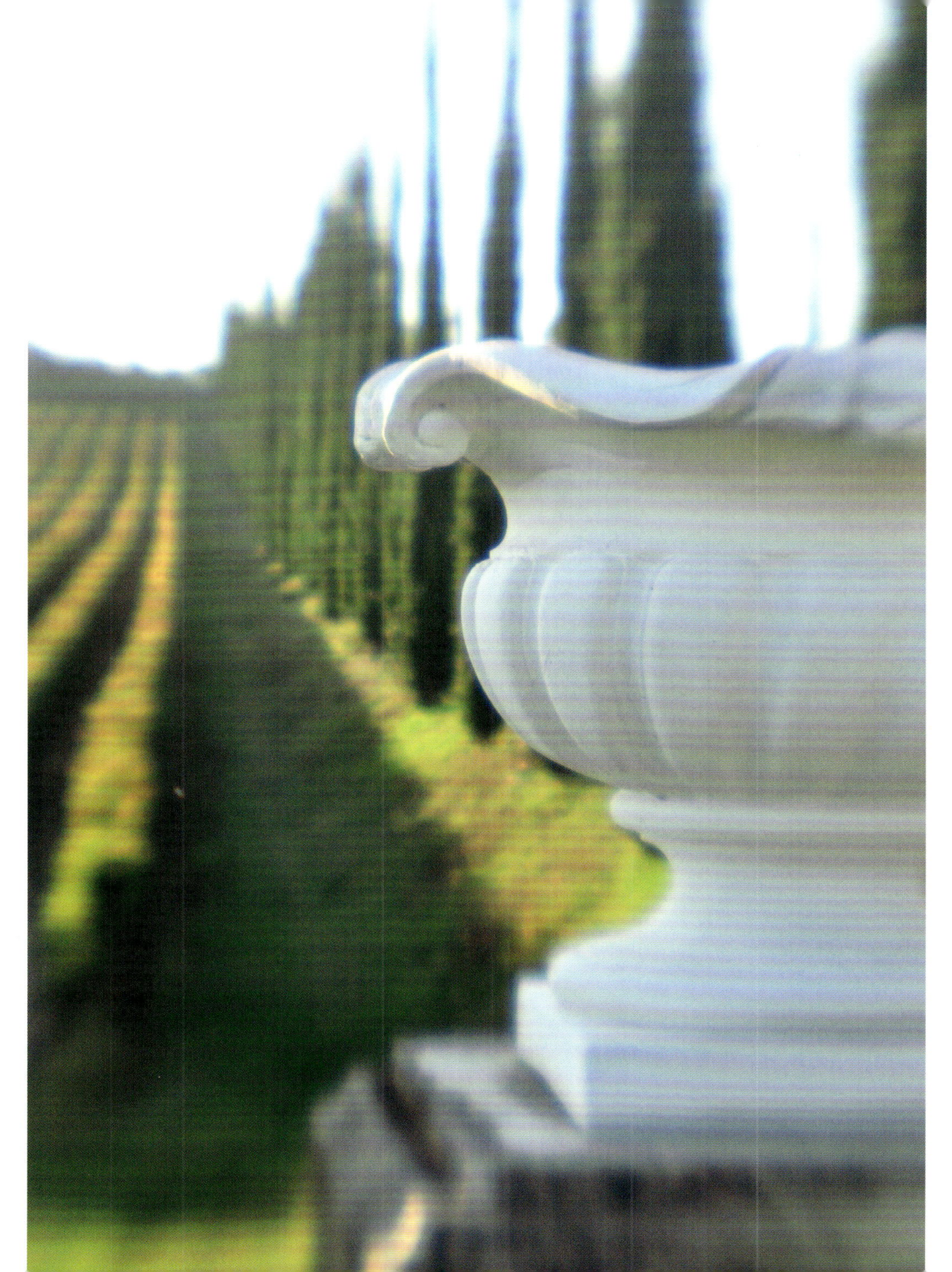

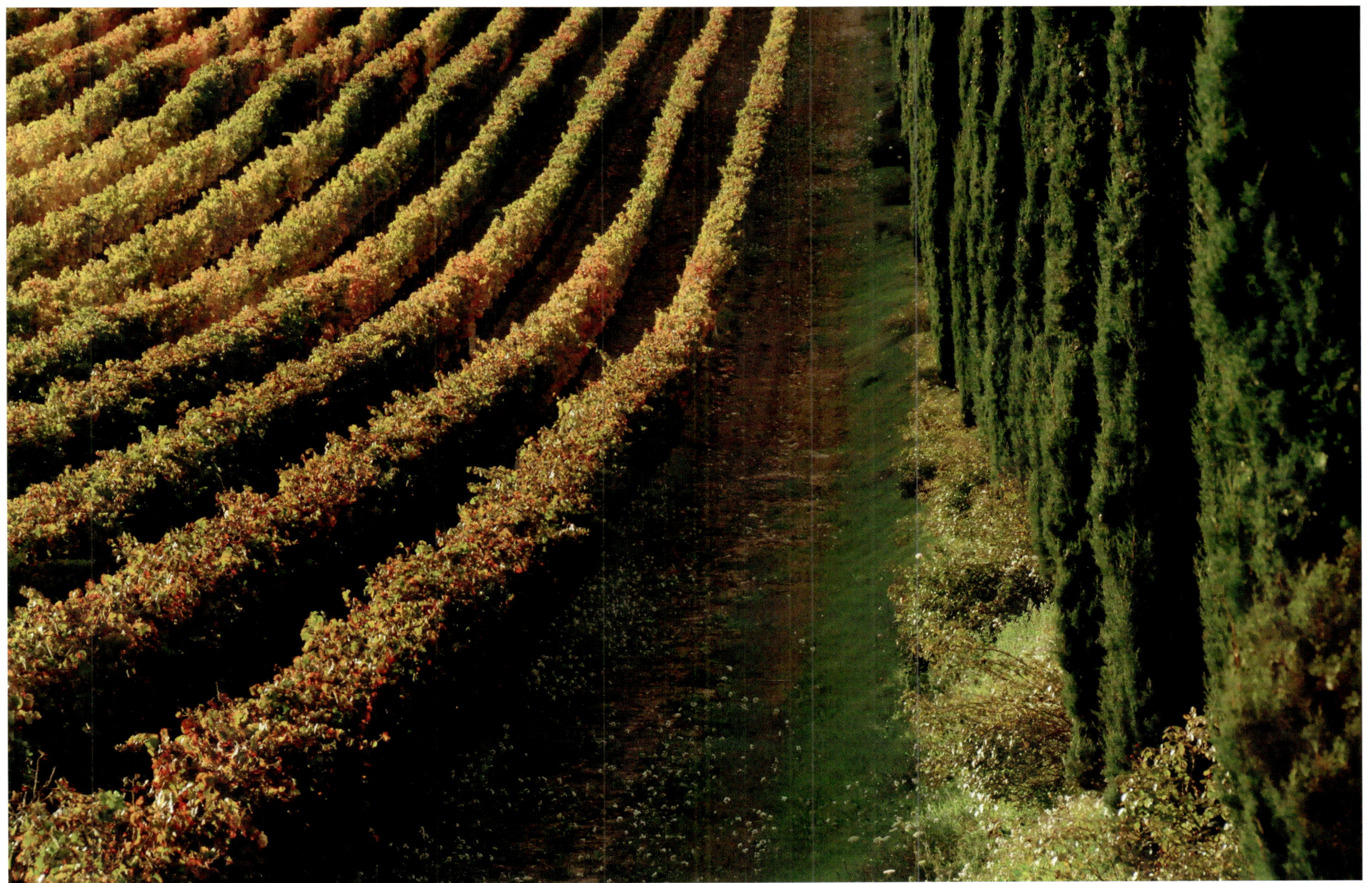

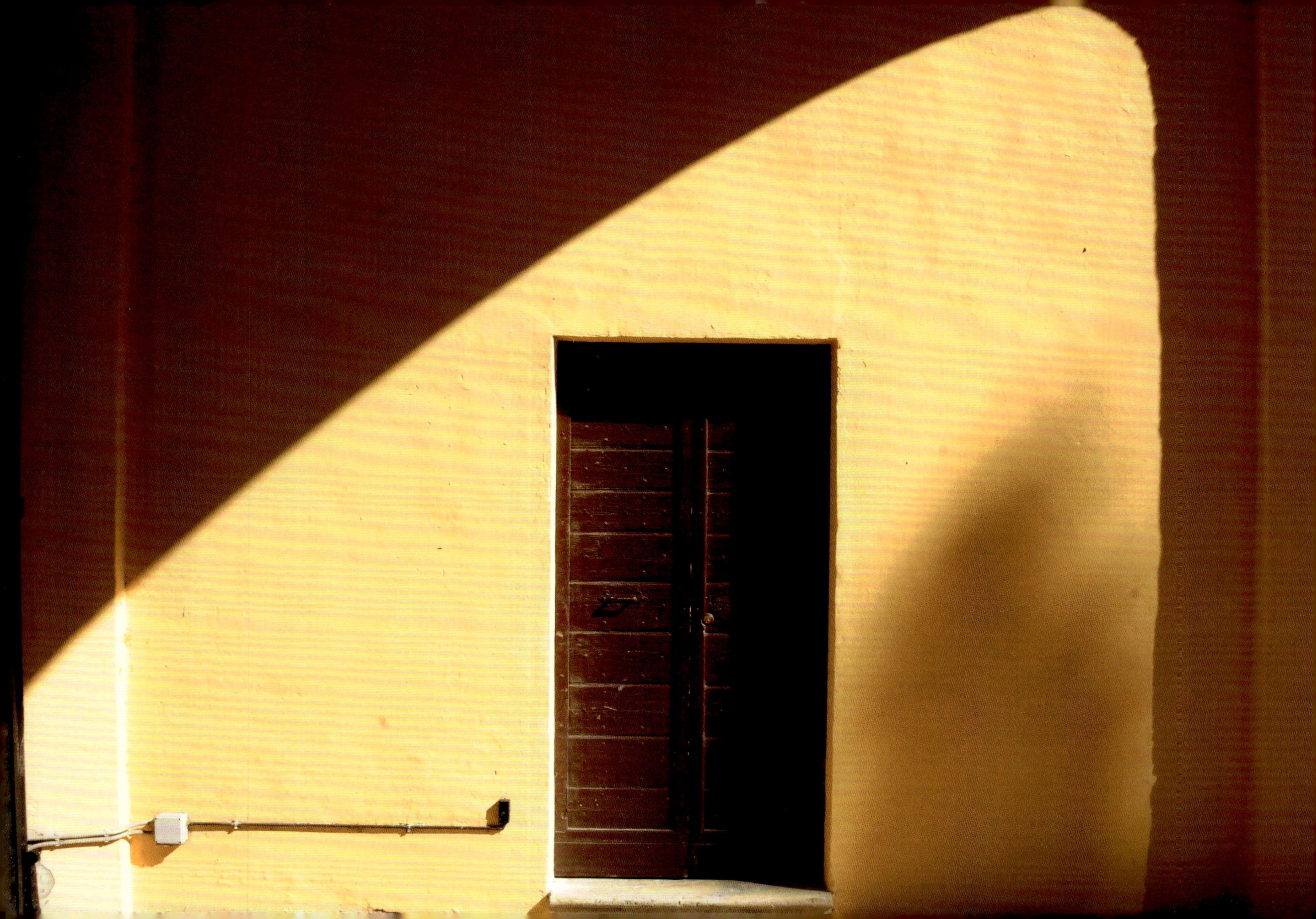

Cannara

Cannara is an unassuming little town divided by a small river that invites leisurely fishing. A small park nearby honors Italian war dead, with a stylized depiction of a fallen soldier looking strikingly like Mussolini. Years ago, the main street featured one supermarket, one gas station, and one ATM. But this is a place that demands you look closer. Cannara was Judy's and my base of operations for our Umbria photo workshops, and La Villa Fattoria del Gelso was our ground zero. There, in this inviting former agriturismo, with a beautiful—and often welcome—fireplace, we lived with our students and formed bonds that have lasted through the years. Across the road was a tiny and photogenic town cemetery. It was always the first stop of our workshop week: an easy walk if one were jet-lagged, with a trove of photo possibilities given the often over-the-top ways Italians honor their beloved dead.

Pork and Chocolate: Porchetta

The CONAD supermarket in the small Umbrian town of Cannara looked like most any supermarket anywhere except for the body of Lenin displayed behind glass in the meat department.

At least, that's what first came to mind when I saw the slow-roasted body of what appeared to be an entire young pig—head, ears, feet—arrayed in a display case, among the more traditional cuts of meat, under a sign bearing the magical word "Porchetta."

In fact, the pig's appendages were decoration; the rest of it was the savory, herb-infused roll of roasted pork belly that is so popular throughout Italy (in multiple permutations) that it is recognized by the Italian government as a traditional food of the country, and therefore of cultural significance.

And no wonder. It's ambrosial, and now international. In New York, Philly, Boston, and any other place that Italian Americans call home, it's often called Italian roast pork, Italian pulled pork, or some variation. But in Italy—especially in central Italy where it was born—it's always porchetta.

What's remarkable about this food is that it is equally renowned—and respected—not only as a main course (especially at the holidays) cut thick and juicy after a long, slow time in the oven—but also as one of the most delicious luncheon meats on the planet, shaved paper thin at room temperature and piled onto crusty Italian rolls, salted, and covered with arugula or other greens. Served thus, no one ever would call this form of porchetta a "leftover."

Judy and I had our first taste of porchetta in 2009 in Treviso, at the start of a promotional tour for our book on Venice in winter. We arrived by train from Venice in the early afternoon, and met our publisher, who promptly took us to lunch with his two adolescent sons, who made it clear to their papa that it was way past lunchtime. Several porchetta sandwiches later, the boys were mollified and Judy and I were smitten.

A few years later our new love for porchetta was sealed three different ways, all in Umbria.

My fondest memory may be from Todi, walking near the Porta Romana doing errands with our friend Doug. It was getting to be late morning and we were getting peckish. Doug made a beeline for the tiny stand near the town's main gate where his friend and neighbor Enrico was slicing and selling his homemade porchetta for sandwiches. Enrico also sold his own cold-pressed olive oil from his 1,000-tree olive grove, literally across the road. It just doesn't get more local—or delicious—than that.

A year or so year later, during market day in Montefalco, we brought our photo students to the town's huge open-air stalls, not just to make photos of all the activity but also to stock up on food we would help make for dinner that evening at our rented villa in Cannara. In the midst of the beautiful radichio, *cippole* (onions), and other *legume* (legumes) was a white wagon (much larger than the one in Todi) bearing the same delicious cargo: porchetta thinly sliced by hand for each customer. None of it, I recall, survived the trip home to Cannara.

It also was in Cannara, during another workshop, that we experienced porchetta at its most elegant. For a number of years we would tour Norcia, the pork capital of Italy, photographing its narrow streets, crowded shops, ancient buildings, and churches. No stop was complete without a visit to Il Richiamo della Sibilla (The Call of the Siren) to watch and photograph proprietor Claudio Lupidi wielding his blade as deftly as a surgeon. (In fact, so respected in ancient times were Norcini (butchers from Norcia) that they occasionally were asked to perform surgery on humans.)

One year, Marco Palermi, our villa's young manager, drove up to join us at Claudio's so he could pick up a beautifully carved pork belly on which Claudio had layered salt, sage, rosemary, thyme, crushed garlic, lemon zest, fennel weed, and who knows what else, then rolled and tied it into a beautiful porchetta, destined to be slow roasted on the villa's indoor fireplace when we returned home. It was our farewell dinner.

And in later years, after the workshop had moved from Cannara to Todi, a succulent roasted porchetta would be the highlight of the welcome dinner at our family-run headquarters hotel. It became for me the good luck charm that all would be well during the coming week.

Pork and Chocolate: Chocolate

Even the most ardent fan can't make a case that Italians "invented" chocolate or, for that matter, coffee or gelato. (Start touting Italian chocolate in superlatives, for example, and pretty soon you'll have Belgians, Germans—not to mention the Swiss—loudly on your case.) Still, for many of these delights—or in coffee's case, necessities—one can argue that Italians have so refined them as to make each their own.

No one, for instance, can shake Italy's claim to gianduja (zhan-DOO-yah) an irresistible combination of chocolate and hazelnut, even if legend credits its invention indirectly to France, and to the economic hardships imposed by the Frenchman every Italian loves to hate: Napoleon Bonaparte.

In 1806 Napoleon, emperor of France and, by dint of his conquests, also king of Italy, instituted what came to be called the Continental System, which prevented British goods from entering European ports under French control.

Though meant to hurt his enemy England, Napoleon's embargo also caused supply shortages in French-ruled countries, especially in the chocolate-producing northern Italian regions of Perugia and Liguria. With stocks of British-transported cacao starting to dwindle, one enterprising chocolatier in Turin thought to mix what remaining chocolate he had with a fine thick paste of ground hazelnuts (nocciole) that were plentiful in the Langhe hills south of the city.

The result was a delicious chocolate-hazelnut butter that could be spread on bread and that was dubbed "gianduja," after a character in the commedia dell'arte—a carefree peasant of the Piedmont countryside known for his tri-corner hat and colorful costume.

Gianduja was an immediate hit, and by the mid-1850s other Italians were using it in other forms, notably gianduiotti, small triangular confections (to mimic Gianduja's tricorn) wrapped in foil.

But that was just the start. It was not long before other chocolatiers, especially in Umbria, created even more incarnations of chocolate and hazelnut, including nocciola truffles, gianduja bars, and arguably the most famous confection of all, Perugina's Baci: little chocolate kisses covered in dark chocolate containing gianduja paste, and a whole roasted hazelnut.

It should not surprise, then, that for the last three decades Perugia, Umbria's capital, has hosted Eurochocolate, a festival of all things chocolate, taking place every fall.

American chocolatier Maria Brandriff remembers:

When I traveled to Umbria in 2011, the only thing that I knew about the town of Perugia was that it was the home of the famous Baci chocolate bonbons. It's a very lovely old walled town which I would have enjoyed thoroughly for its history and architecture had not a major chocolate festival sprouted overnight on the main piazza.

As a chocolatier, I was amazed and delighted . . . the entire center square of the town was filled with white tented stalls filled with various types of chocolate confections, and the air was sweetly redolent of chocolate. There were all sorts of bars and bonbons, chocolate drinks, chocolate gelato and even, as a bit of entertainment, a mime completely covered in chocolate. Alas, I did not have the opportunity to test whether it was, indeed, real chocolate!

My first thought was, How much room do I have in my suitcase and how much product can I bring home? I struck gold when I discovered an entire booth devoted to gianduja. . . . In the States it's quite difficult to come by, so I promptly purchased about a five pound bar. . . . Every Christmas holiday season I make hundreds of chocolate truffles for family and friends. One of the most popular flavors that I produce, I happen to call Better than Baci The filling is a blend of gianduja, dark chocolate, Frangelico, and cream. No more internet hunts for that elusive ingredient.

So what about Nutella?

Comparing Nutella to gianduja may be like comparing a frozen supermarket pizza to one made by hand in Napoli. Still, there is no denying its phenomenal, worldwide popularity. Now composed mostly of sugar and palm oil, Nutella was invented after World War II by a baker from the Piedmont named Pietro Ferrero, who conjured yet another chocolate-hazelnut paste that could easily be spread on bread. In 1951 he called it Supercrema Gianduja. Like its predecessors, it took off like a rocket.

In later years, Ferrero's son Michele changed the recipe, with an eye toward wider European distribution—and wider profits. He changed the Supercrema name to Nutella. Today, Nutella is only 13% hazelnuts and contains no actual chocolate, only cocoa powder. But don't tell that to Italian schoolkids, who look forward to their afternoon snack of Nutella on toast almost as much as their parents crave their first Moka-pot espresso in the morning.

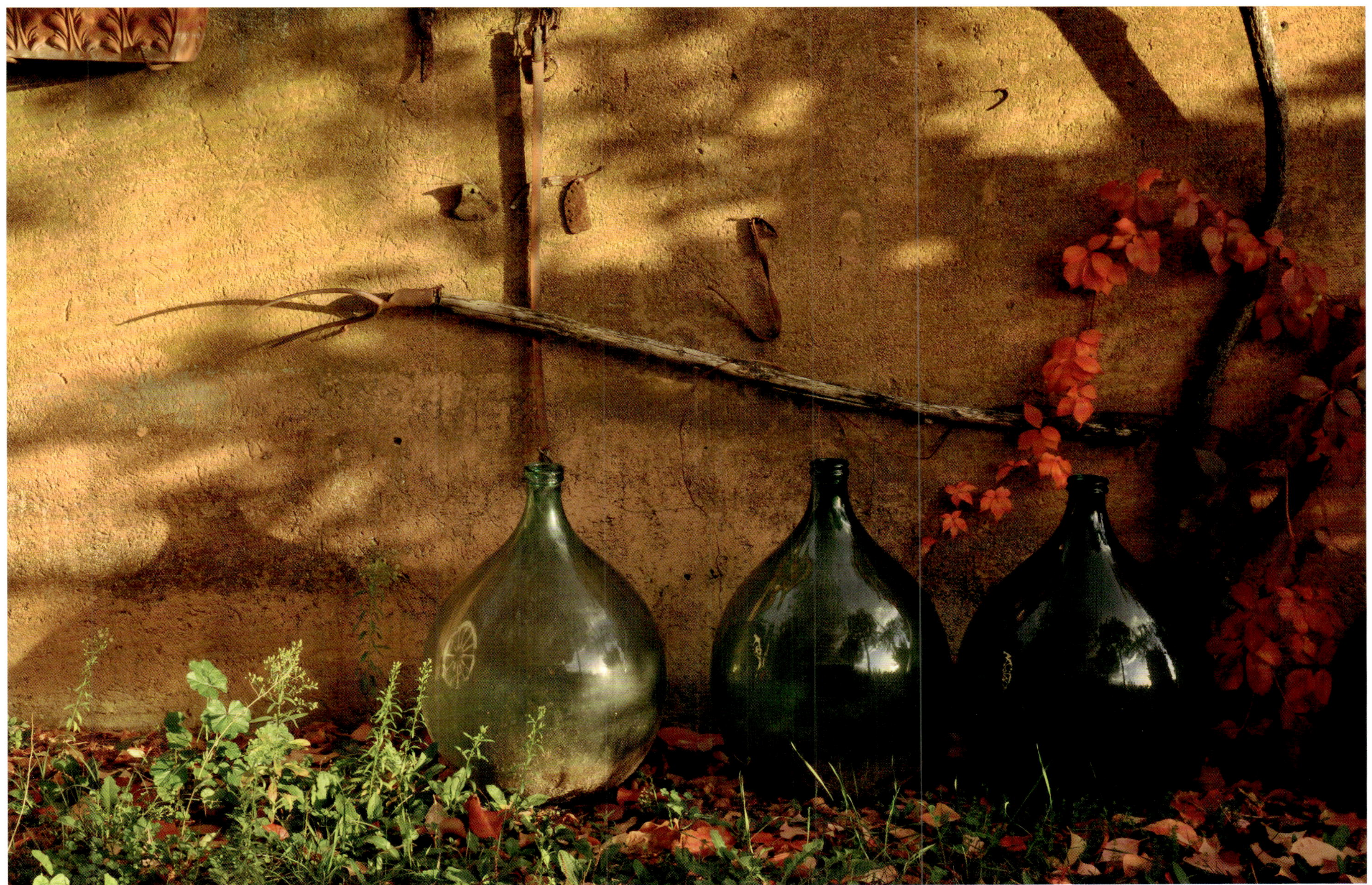

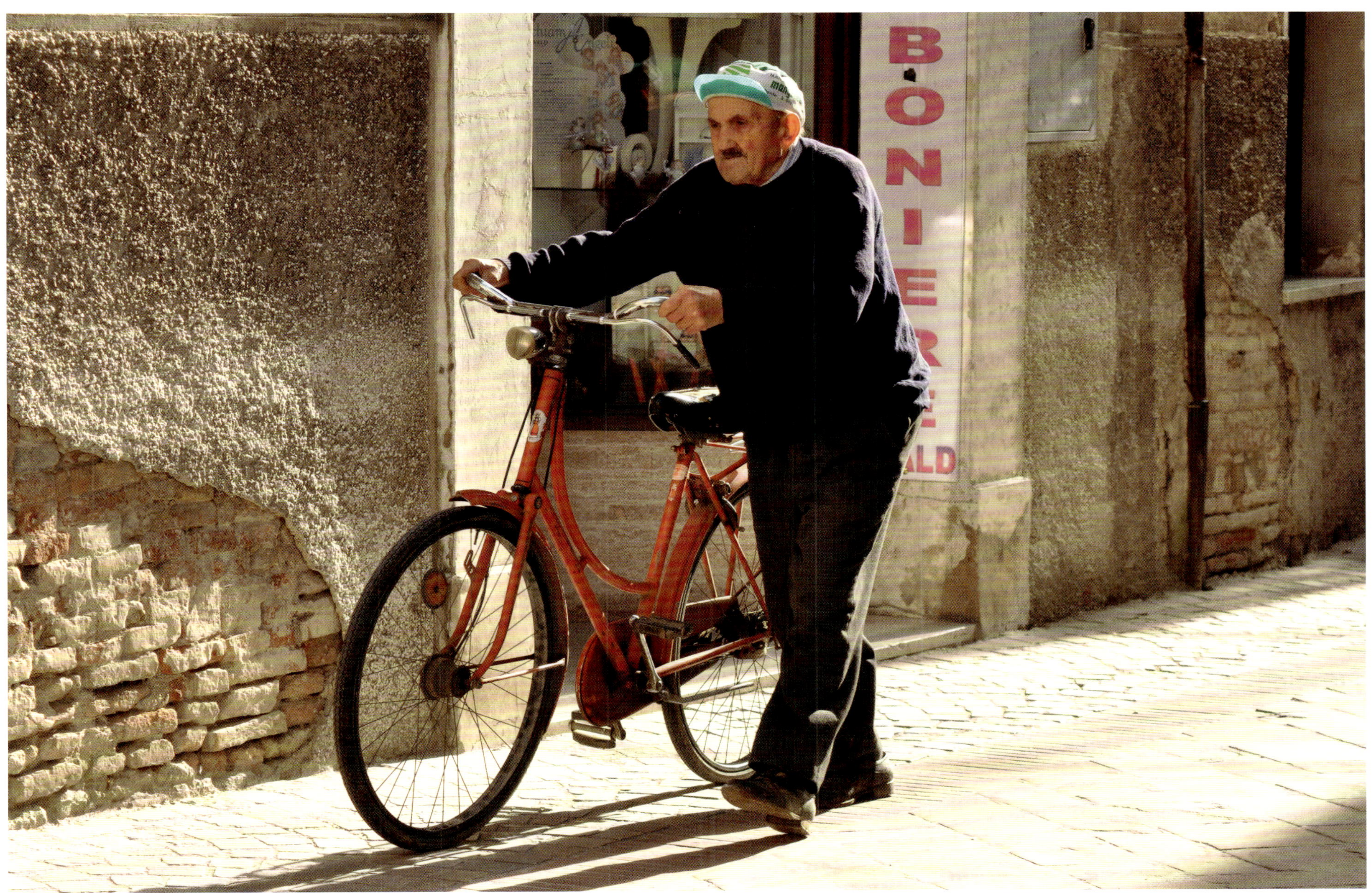

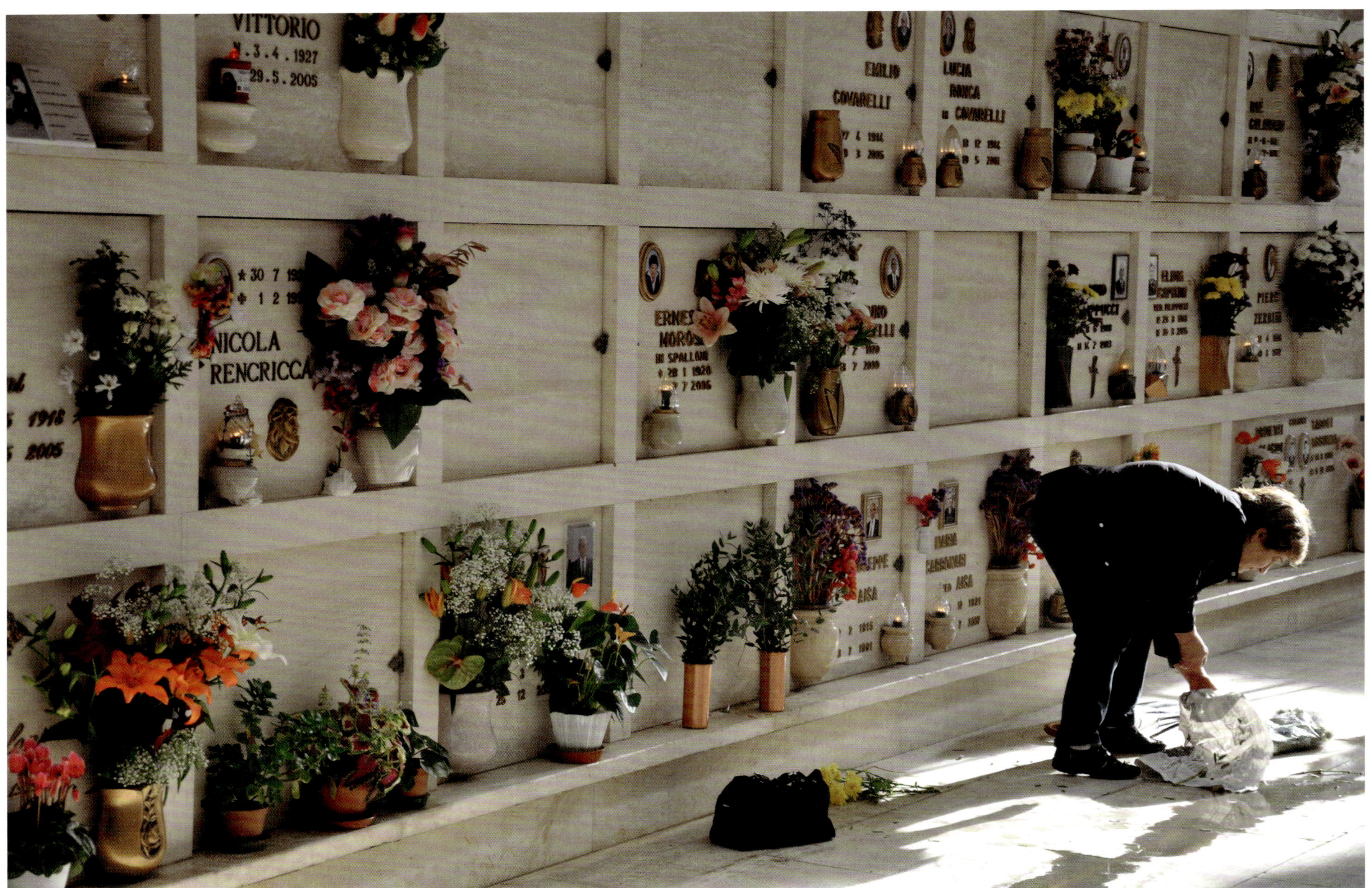
VITTORIO
N. 3. 4. 1927
29. 5. 2005
EMILIO
COVARELLI
LUCIA
RONCA
in COVARELLI
NICOLA
RENCRICCA

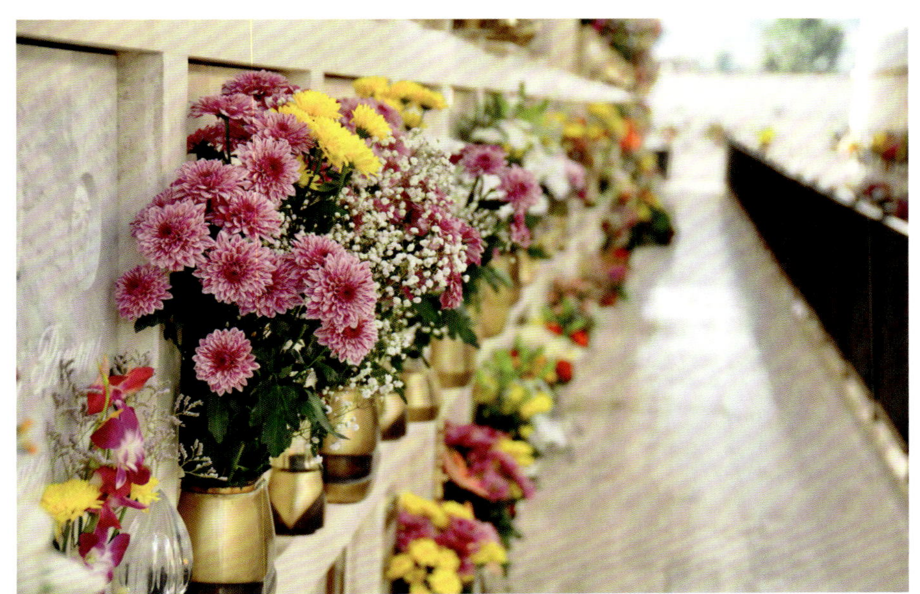

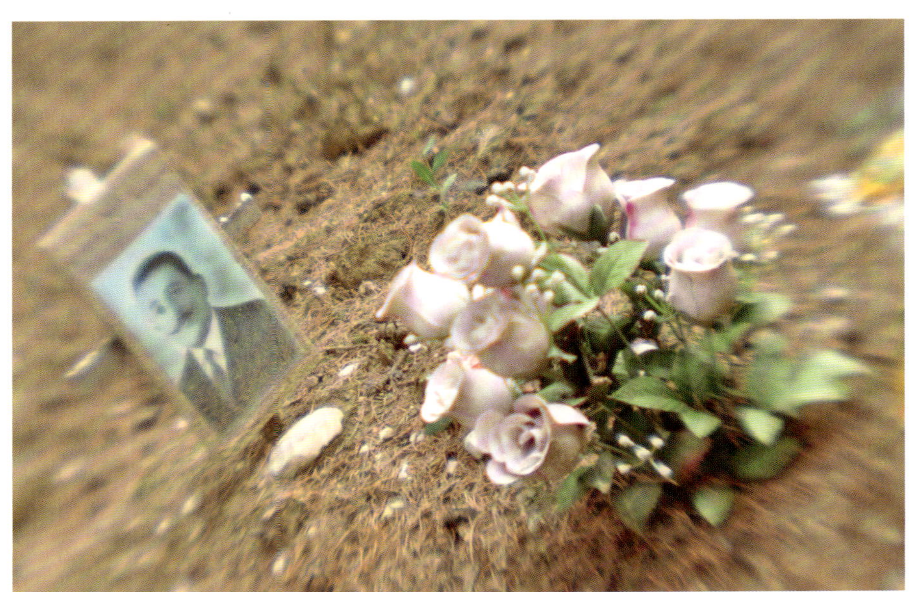

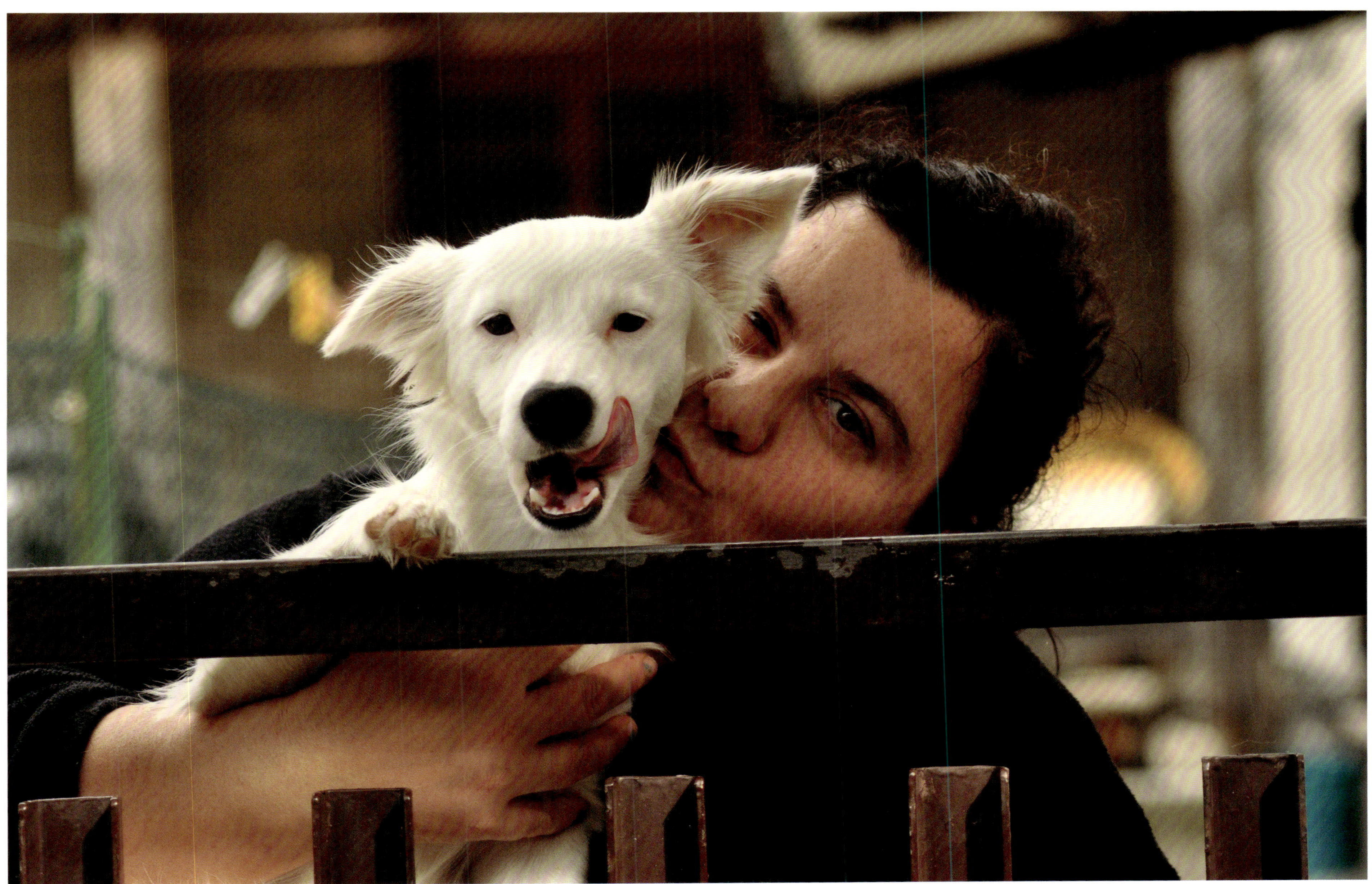

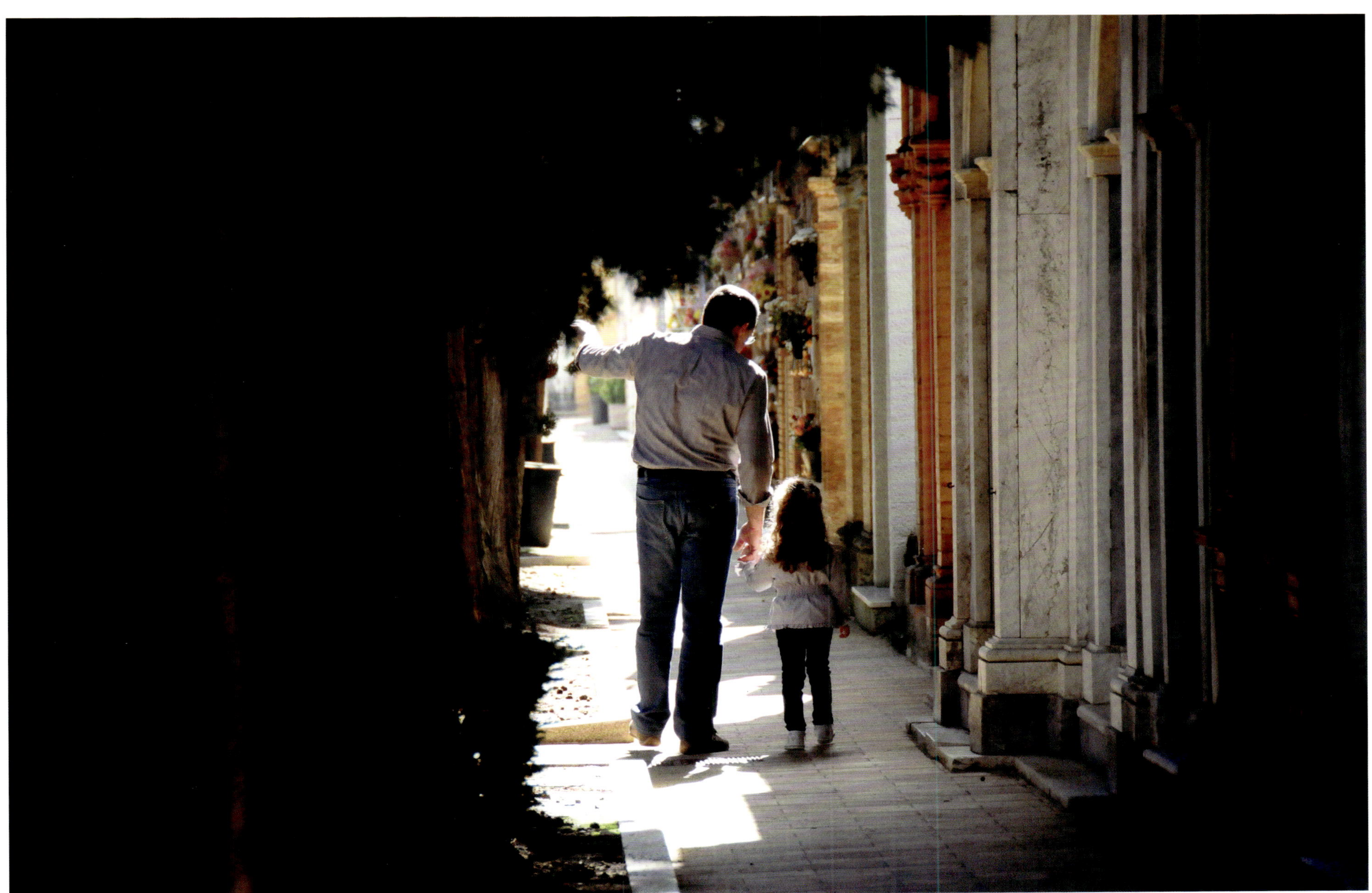

Vignettes

Pre-Black & Decker in Assisi

There is much to ogle in Assisi's Basilica di San Francesco, the magnificent two-church tribute to St. Francis, built one atop the other, and finished in 1367, 141 years after the friar's death.

Each year pilgrims and the merely curious flock by the thousands to the basilica—with its soaring nave and subterranean chapel featuring Francis's crypt—and are overwhelmed by the nave's brilliant lapis-lazuli starry sky, not to mention gloriously ornate portraits, brilliant gold leaf and, of course, the famous series of Giotto frescoes lining the nave's lower walls that depict the life of St. Francis.

Giotto was a young apprentice of the fourteenth-century master Cimabue and worked under him during the decoration of the basilica. When Cimabue left Assisi to work on another commission, Giotto took over leading his team of artists.

You can't enter the nave without being overwhelmed. If you are religious, you also can't help but thank your personal deity for preserving this space after the second in a series of deadly earthquakes in 1997 took the lives of four people inspecting the damage from the first one. (Inevitably, video of this second earthquake now is viewable on YouTube.) The fully restored nave, resurrecting thousands of pieces of fresco as if from a giant jigsaw puzzle is, surely, a modern artistic miracle.

Yet equally miraculous to me is a work that was completed in 1501 by master woodcarver Domenico Indovini. A brilliant example of carving and inlay, Indovini's 102-seat choir stall sits below the nave's wonderful ceiling and, unlike the Giotto frescoes, can be viewed up close. Every inlay, every curve, every wooden vine, every floret offers itself to the viewer in astounding detail.

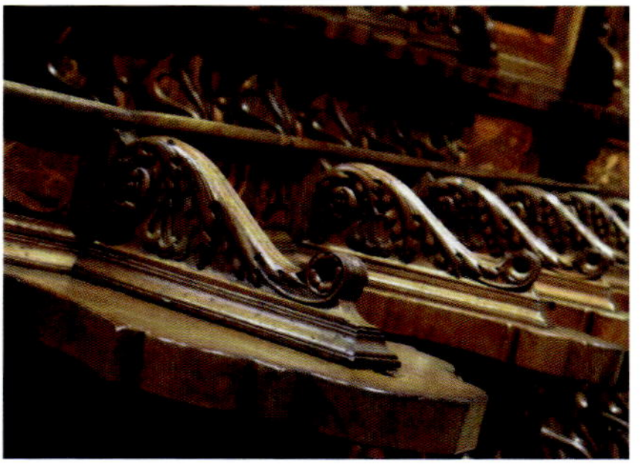

The project took Indovini and his team a decade to finish—all without power tools.

Citta dei Morti

Cannara is a pleasing interruption on a state road, just a few miles from Assisi. On one side is a high-banked stream and public park. It also has an impressive, if also human-scale, cemetery on the edge of town right near the villa we once used for our photo workshops. During those early years, when the *studenti* were battling jet lag on their first full day in Umbria, it was an easy first stop, right after breakfast and walking distance from the villa.

There's something about Italian cemeteries—whether huge, like il Cimitero in Venice, or much smaller like Cannara's, that compels attention. Italians often celebrate their dead in elaborate family mausoleums, while standard cemetery plots feature intricately carved gravestones and headstones, all attended by multitudes of flowers, trees, and shrubbery.

In Cannara local families visit regularly, sometimes every Sunday, and include the children, who seem to know how to behave. The sheer variety of the mausoleums, walkable on tree-shaded pathways, range from starkly modern to Baroque. They follow absolutely no pattern and are a visual feast. The more modern section of the cemetery, behind the century-old front gateway and small chapel, is literally a City of the Dead where funeral urns rest out of sight in row upon row of small marble vaults stacked two stories high and blocks deep, accessible by movable library stairs. In other places, this could look sterile, but this is Italy and each vault is decorated, not just with abundant flowers but with framed photos of the departed and, just as often, with loving words.

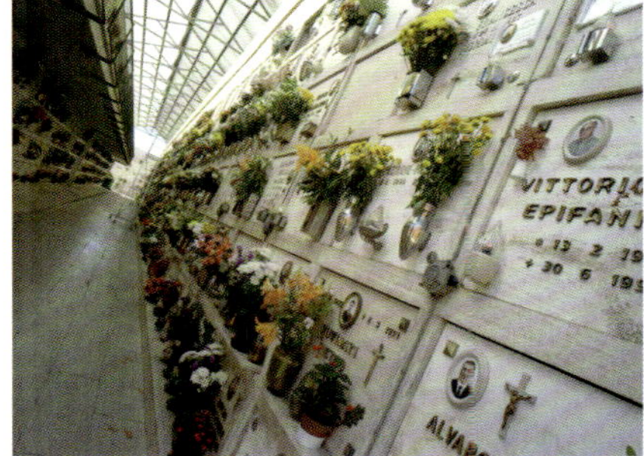

Gelato as Health Food

Gelato tastes richer and creamier than ice cream because it contains less, not more, butterfat (5–8% versus a *minimum* of 10% for ice cream—often much more). This intensifies gelato's natural flavors. It also is churned less so it is denser, creating a more luxurious mouthfeel. Bottom line: gelato is better than ice cream—and better for you.

I doubt whether most Italians take this into account during their evening passeggiata, when searching for a frozen treat. Still, as an American, I take comfort in the fact that, when scarfing down a cup of nocciola, at least I am not scarfing down Rocky Road.

In fact, there is no right time to enjoy gelato, though I can't say I've actually eaten it for breakfast. (I've come close, though.) In fact, it was in Rome in 1970 (on my first honeymoon) that I first fell in love with real gelato—hazelnut, or nocciola, quickly becoming my favorite. But it was in Venice (on my second honeymoon), and finally in Umbria, where I got to sample the complete richness of gelato's flavor palette.

In and around Todi's Piazza del Popolo there are several gelaterie, each serving homemade and wonderful product. But it was a hole-in-the-wall place, Gelateria Pianegiani, a few blocks from the piazza and down the hill from our hotel, that stole my gelato-loving heart.

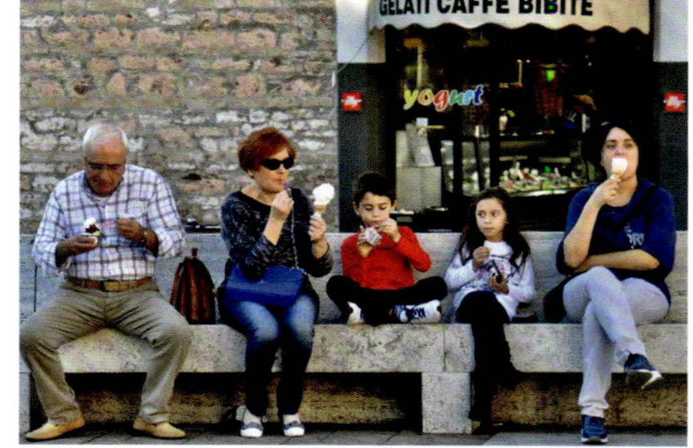

The place is tiny, which seems to add to its homey appeal. There are sumptuous pastries as well, though honestly I always went there with a single mission. Of course hazelnut, but the chocolate! I've never seen gelato so dark—the darkest, richest chocolate brown I ever have seen, much less tasted. Not to mention stracciatella, fior di latte, or pistacchio. Our nearby hotel, the Fonte Cesia, handed out discount coupons to Pianegiani saying we would not be disappointed.

Talk about a win-win. And so healthy, too.

Segway Nonna

Bevagna remains one of our favorite towns in Umbria, and not just because it has one of our very favorite restaurants, Le Delizie del Borgo, run by chef-owner Simone Proietti Pesci.

Le Delizie became our go-to place for lunch with our photo students after we first met Simone, a short bearded man with a twinkling gaze and a genius for turning local specialties like guanciale, black truffles, and handmade gnocchi into glorious, though never fussy, meals.

Even without Simone's restaurant, located in a lovely park just outside Bevagna's medieval walls, we would love the town for its quirky car-free vibe, its curving stone walkways, soaring views, and welcoming people.

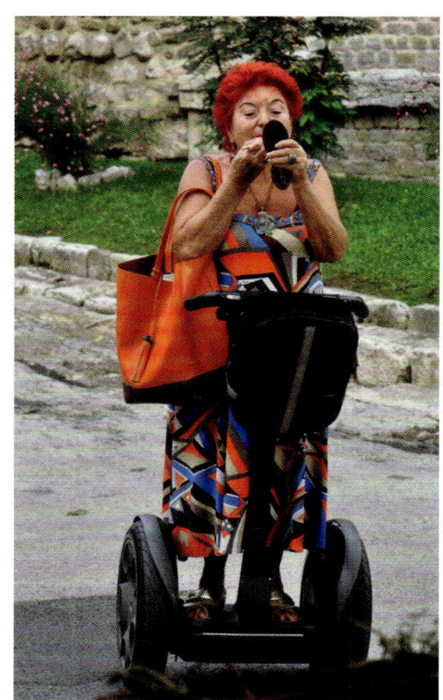

Though small, the town opens up onto several lovely squares where, on any given day, one might see boys and girls playing a raucous game of tag, or where locals sit on the steps of several churches chatting. (This also is the town where we first saw chairs set out in front of shops to allow seniors to sit a spell.)

One year, at a small outdoor flea market, Judy, who is an assemblage sculptor, was fascinated by a small homemade animal trap (similar to Havaharts in the States but way more rustic). We shipped it home and now it is the centerpiece of a lovely artwork.

But who would have thought of a Segway-riding nonna in a place dating back to the Middle Ages?

Yet there she was, in a brightly colored dress—and outrageously red hair—adjusting her makeup on the contraption, with considerable, and well-balanced, aplomb.

Somehow, in Bevagna, it seemed right.

Art Restorer / Rock Drummer

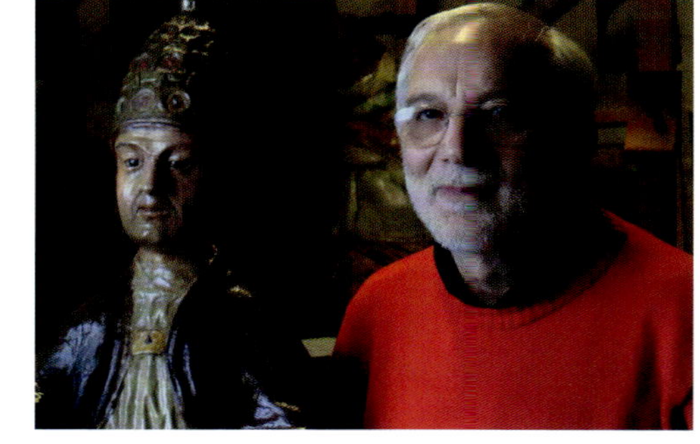

Todi, supposedly the world's most livable city, seems to protect itself from malign outside influence by ringing itself with not one but three sets of ancient walls, expanding outward with passing centuries.

And it is interesting to experience not just what happens behind those walls but inside them as well.

These walls are huge. And wide. Not like something thrown together by a weekend gardener to set off the hostas from the geraniums.

You can, for example, live in them—like Doug and Debbie Badger. Their Todi retreat is literally built within Todi's thick outer wall and, while one never would call their cozy four-story home huge, it certainly is spacious, even if Debbie, one of the best cooks I know, probably longs for a larger kitchen (who doesn't?).

The secret life of Todi's walls came home to me when we visited a local art restorer in his (literally) cavernous studio.

The first thing I noticed was the absence of windows—built inside a wall, remember—but the carved-out interior space had easily been wired for electricity and light. The walls of the artisan's huge workroom were, as you would expect, rough-hewn stone, and I do recall the presence of, if not dampness, then perhaps a slight humidity. Any number of ancient artworks—from paintings to huge church crucifixes to wooden sculpture—awaited his scrutiny, probably benefiting from the higher relative humidity as they prepared to achieve their former glory. I made a portrait of the restorer next to a worn wooden sculpture of a bejeweled cleric. I did it by available light—only this time the light that was available came from a huge rectangular work light, balanced for daylight, in a stone room where there was none.

At the end of the visit, the artist showed us around his space, including an unprepossessing side room that could have been used for storage. But inside this room, set up and ready to rock, was a complete drum kit. The man obviously had a side hustle, and in his sanctum sanctorum, he never had to worry about making too much noise.

What's in a Name?

Doug Badger is as Italian as I am—which is to say we each have Italian mothers. But non-Italian surnames coupled with non-Italian first names can lend themselves to, shall we say, colorful pronunciation.

One year, we were unable to see Doug and his wife, Debbie, for our usual dinner and overnight at their place in Todi before we left to hook up with our workshop students in Cannara. No problem, they said; we'll leave a key for you.

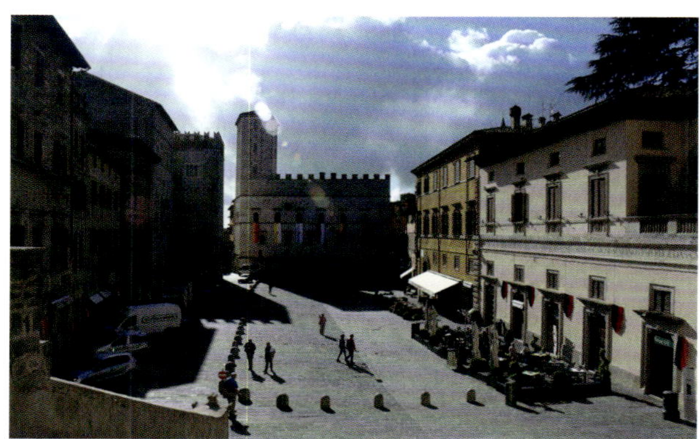

All they asked was that, when we left, we drop off our bedsheets at the local laundry, where they had an account.

Doug had warned me that the locals had a hard time pronouncing his name. "Doug Badger" came out sounding like "Dark Baggio."

After our stay, Judy and I dropped off the sheets at the nearby laundry, but I forgot what Doug had told me.

"Doug Badger," I said, handing over the bed linen. Blank stare.

"Dark Baggio," I corrected myself.

"Ah!" came the smiling reply.

How Green Was My Olive Oil

Chauvinistically, as a half-Italian kid growing up in New York, with plenty of Italian relatives in New Jersey, I thought most olive oil—a staple in every Italian kitchen I knew—came from Italy. I was wrong.

Most of the world's olive oil comes from Spain. In fact, Italy accounts for a mere 15% of the total world production each year.

Not only that, but look closely at that big bottle of Italian EVOO in your pantry and chances are the fine print will say that the oil therein comes from Italy—as well as from Greece, Portugal, Spain, or Tunisia. (This is legal under current European Union regulations.)

But at least it's all olive oil, right?

Sometimes. The sad fact is that a surprising percentage of Italian premium olive oil sold in the US has been adulterated—with lesser olive oil, canola oil, who knows what—to make the product exponentially more profitable for the producers to export to a gullible American market.

But the other side of this story is Umbria. "Umbria oil makes up only 2% of Italy's olive oil production, but wins a far larger proportion of awards" in culinary competitions, notes journalist and author Elaine Sciolino. After all, a big part of what makes Italy's green heart green are Umbria's olives: especially the assertive, peppery moraiolo olives that produce its very best extra virgin oils. These Umbrian oils are produced in comparatively small quantity—at least compared to the mega-labels familiar in America—and to some, may be an acquired taste.

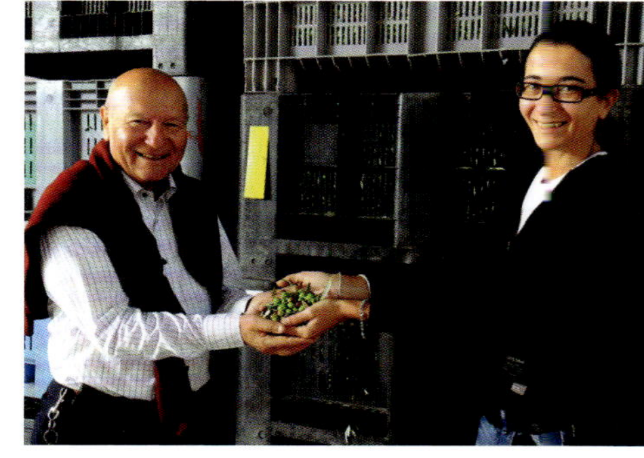

These are oils, after all, that should never be used for cooking. They are instead a condiment, an embellishment—an adornment—poured in a heavy green drizzle over a salad, or even better, over a steaming bowl of pappa al pomodoro.

"You should feel piquant on the tip of your tongue and bitter deep in your throat," noted one olive-oil producer. "It is full of antioxidants that make it aggressive. You are not in the sweetness of Tuscany here."

So you can imagine our delight at the package we received just before the holidays some years ago, from Marco Palermi, the caretaker of our rented villa in Cannara. Marco was shipping Judy the rustic animal trap that she had bought at a flea market in Bevagna to be used in one of her sculptures. But the package was much heavier than we expected.

Inside was an unmarked five-liter can full of freshly pressed, *tanto robusto*, Umbrian olive oil—from Marco's father's olive trees.

Christmas came early that year.

Afterword

Am I looking at Umbria through prosecco-tinted glasses?

That always is a danger when a non-native waxes poetic about a place he or she has come to love. I probably have approached that with a number of other places, and in several other books: the Chesapeake, Down East Maine, Paris, Venice. But I hope in all these cases that my words, and now our pictures, have shown a version of truth or at least verisimilitude.

Still, would I love and celebrate the Italians' embrace of a three-hour lunch or a four-hour dinner were I an underpaid office worker in Torino or a night-shift taxi driver in Rome?

Probably not.

If putting food on the table depended at least in part on the Italian welfare state, would I—could I—spend time contemplating art or architecture in Orvieto or Assisi or, for that matter, pass time watching how the sun plays on a hillside in Todi or Cannara?

Again, probably not.

Still, our perspective as American visitors brings with it, by definition, new eyes and, one hopes, new appreciation.

For an American inured to the mediocrity of McDonald's and the sterility of Starbucks, a new morning ritual of a perfectly pulled cappuccino and a freshly made cornetto—enjoyed at a sunlit table in Todi's Piazza del Popolo, for example—can form a metaphor for what makes this part of the world remarkable.

Watching meticulous women in Gubbio and Deruta using impossibly tiny brushes to decorate vases and dinnerware one by one might trigger something in our brains about our disposable society.

And simply observing so many people in so many of these towns and cities treating their ancient surroundings with respect—even love—especially in a postpandemic reopening, you can't help but appreciate their innate regard for their history and gratitude for where they live.

I grant that tourists (or documentary photographers) too often can view simpatico things like these at a romantic remove. Yet I would add that, precisely because of where we Americans are on the world food chain, some of us also can appreciate how a society based largely on the bottom line can distort not only the quality of life of a person, but of a country as well.

And for that, bella Umbria, we thank you for the gentle, delightful—corrective—experience that you have given us.

—Frank Van Riper and Judith Goodman, Washington, DC; Lubec, Maine

Acknowledgments

In mid-2008, as our first joint book, *Serenissima: Venice in Winter*, neared publication, I ventured, book dummy in hand, into Bella Italia, a high-end Italian gift shop in Bethesda, Maryland.

Taking one look at the dummy, co-owner Suzy Menard immediately offered Judy and me a fall book signing to coincide with the shop's tenth anniversary.

We didn't know it then, but that also was the beginning of our next joint book, *The Green Heart of Italy: Umbria and Its Ancient Neighbors*.

Over dinner after the first of what would be three sell-out book events, Suzy and her husband, Bill, regaled us with stories about Umbria, where they owned a villa, La Fattoria del Gelso, near the tiny Umbrian hill town of Cannara. For several years thereafter, their villa became the headquarters for our first international photography workshops, and the base from which Judy and I fell in love with this beautiful, verdant, simpatico region.

Doing a book that twins original photography with original text requires not only being there—preferably over a period of years to do it right—but also lots of long-form research and interviews. And that requires access. During the course of our work, the following people, in Italy and the United States, were generous with their time, hospitality, recommendations, and friendship, for which Judy and I always will be grateful: During the nearly ten years that we taught in Umbria, Doug and Debbie Badger, dear friends and fellow Italophiles, welcomed us to their second home in Todi (on our way to Cannara). Later, when we needed a new base of operations for our workshops, they suggested Todi and the small, elegant Hotel Fonte Cesia, literally at the top of the town. This family-run haven welcomed us and our students like old friends, and we thank them all.

While based in Todi, we also were fortunate to have tour guide Elisa Picchiotti get us into places in this gorgeous town that the average tourist never sees. (It also was Elisa who revealed to me how the town's lovely main square—suitably aged for the occasion—had substituted for ancient Rome in the 1965 film *The Agony and the Ecstasy*.)

Of all the wonderful places in which we ate, Le Delizie del Borgo in Bevagna was our favorite, not just for the food but for the gracious welcome we always received from chef/owner Simone Proietti Pesci. Lunch at Le Delizie was always a highlight of our workshop week. We were introduced to Simone by Suzy and Bill Menard.

Back in the States, Judy and I ran into our old friend artist Daphne Taylor one summer in Lubec, Maine, where we each had second homes. Bringing our friend up to date on our book in progress, she immediately suggested we talk to her former art-school colleague Yarrott Benz.

Decades ago, Daphne said, Benz, then a newly minted MFA in sculpture, had been an assistant to Beverly Pepper, the late American sculptor, when she and her journalist husband lived in Todi, and where she had a sculpture studio. I reached Yarrott by phone and spent hours conversing in person and over email soaking up his recollections of working with one of the greatest sculptors of her generation. I am proud of the resultant chapter, filled with color and personal reminiscences.

Finally, we once again thank the team at Daylight Books, publishers of my previous book, on New York and Paris: Publisher Michael Itkoff, Creative Director Ursula Damm, and Copy Editor Gabrielle Fastman.

After the superb job Daylight did producing *Recovered Memory: New York & Paris 1960–1980*, it was hard for me to think they could surpass themselves.

They did.

Judy and I could not have done this book without these gracious and talented colleagues and friends. In book publishing, as in life, it takes a village.

Tantissime grazie a tutti.

—FVR and JG

List of Plates

97: Hillside Villa / Orvieto

98: Exuberant Girl / Bevagna

103: Civita di Bagnoregio

105: Elegant Square / Bevagna

106–107: Anziani / Bevagna

109: Church / Civita di Bagnoeregio

110: Town Fountain (2) / Bevagna

111: Religious Procession / Bevagna

112: Green Walkway / Bevagna

114: Olive Harvest; Ragazzo / Bevagna

115: Pastoral Vineyard / Bevagna

117: Sagrantino, Cypress

118: Abstract / Cannara Cemetery

123: Wine Jugs / Cannara

125: Bike Rider / Bevagna

126–127: Burial Vaults; Cemetery Details / Cannara

129: Bacio per Cane Felice

131: Cemetery Visit / Cannara

132: Choir Stall Detail / Assisi

133: Burial Vaults / Cannara

134: Enjoying Gelato / Assisi

135: Segway Nonna / Bevagna

136: Art Restorer / Todi

137: Piazza del Popolo / Todi

138: Father-Daughter Olive Oil Makers

148: Umbria Vista

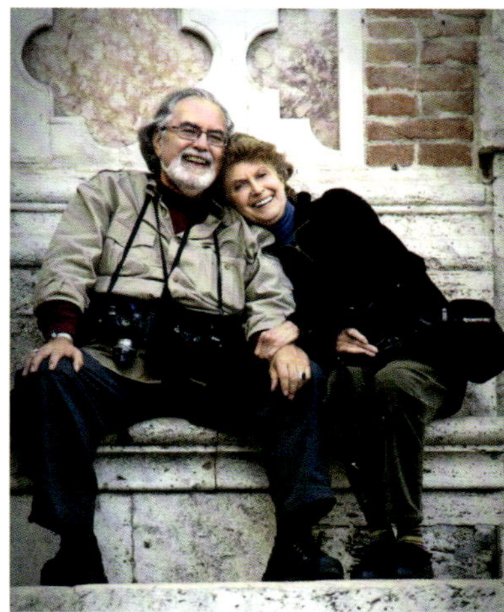

Credit: Fritz Gibbon

Frank Van Riper and **Judith Goodman** are husband-and-wife documentary and fine-art photographers whose work has been published internationally. Goodman's photography has hung in the Corcoran Gallery of Art in Washington, DC, and the Baltimore Museum; she also is an award-winning assemblage sculptor and a member of the Washington Sculptors' Group. Van Riper's photography is in the permanent collections of the National Portrait Gallery (Washington, DC) as well as the Portland Gallery of Art (Portland, Maine). His 1998 book of photography and essays, *Down East Maine/A World Apart*, was nominated for a Pulitzer Prize and won the Silver Award for photography from the Art Directors Club of Metropolitan Washington. His most recent book is *Recovered Memory: New York & Paris 1960–1980.*

Goodman and Van Riper are the coauthors of *Serenissima: Venice in Winter* (2008), an internationally best-selling coffee-table book of black-and-white photographs and essays that was published in the United States and in Italy.

Frank Van Riper also is a widely read online photography columnist (www.TalkingPhotography.com) and for nineteen years was the photography columnist of the *Washington Post*. Before that he served as White House correspondent, national political correspondent, and Washington Bureau news editor of the *New York Daily News*. He was a 1979 Nieman Fellow at Harvard and holds the 1980 Merriman Smith Award (with the late Lars-Erik Nelson) from the White House Correspondents' Association.

Van Riper is a popular teacher and lecturer, and is on the faculty of Photoworks at Glen Echo Park, Maryland. He has lectured widely, including at the Maine Photographic Workshops and the Smithsonian Resident Associate program. In 2007 he was awarded the Distinguished Achievement Award from the University of Maine at Machias for his "outstanding career in journalism and photography" and in 2011 was inducted into the City College of New York Communications Alumni Hall of Fame.

Goodman and Van Riper have jointly taught photography workshops in the US and in Italy: The Lubec Photo Workshops at SummerKeys (Lubec, Maine) and, in Italy, the Umbria Photo Workshops, as well as Unseen Serenissima: The Venice in Winter Photo Workshops (www.GVRphoto.com).

They live in Washington, DC.

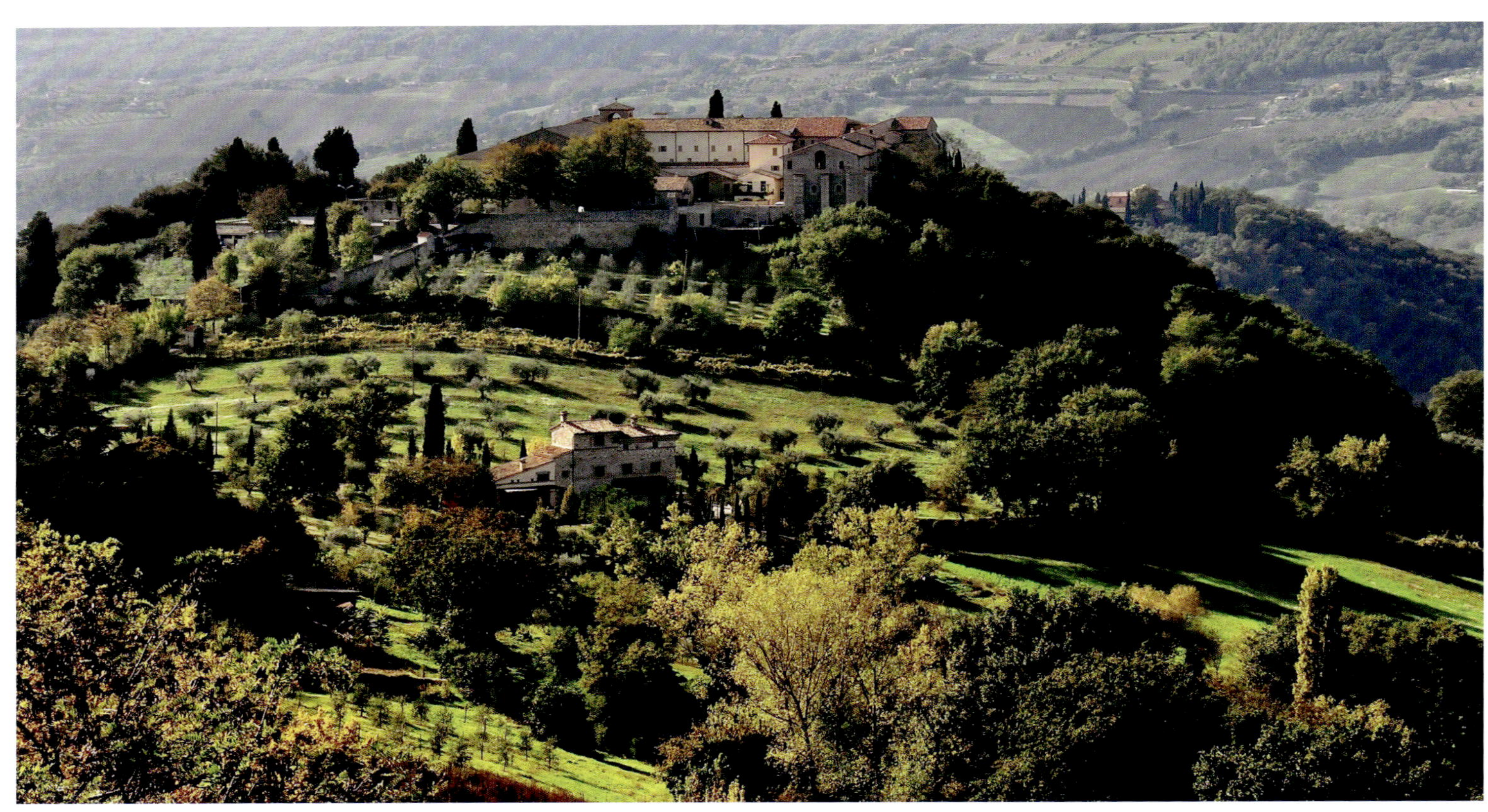